CULTURE & LANGUAGE ACQUISITION

AN INTRODUCTION TO WORLDVIEW AND GUIDE INTO LEARNING A NEW LANGUAGE AND CULTURE

20 TUTORIALS WITH DISCUSSION
POINTS AND ACTIVITIES

ACCESSTRUTH

Culture and Language Acquisition
An introduction to worldview and learning a new language & culture
Communication Foundations, Module 6 of the Cross-Cultural Essentials Curriculum

Copyright © 2019 AccessTruth

Version 1.0

ISBN: 978-0-6484151-4-5

Published by AccessTruth
PO Box 8087
Baulkham Hills NSW 2153
Australia

Email: info@accesstruth.com
Web: accesstruth.com

Cover and interior design by Matthew Hillier
Edited by Simon Glover

Table of Contents

About the Cross-Cultural Essentials Curriculum

It's no secret that there are still millions of people in the world living in "unreached" or "least-reached" areas. If you look at the maps, the stats, and the lists of people group names, it's almost overwhelming. The people represented by those numbers can't find out about God, or who Jesus Christ is, or what He did for them because there's no Bible in their language or church in their area – they have *no access* to Truth.

So you could pack a suitcase and jump on a plane, but then what? How would you spend your first day? How would you start learning language? When would you tell them about Jesus? Where would you start? The truth is that a mature, grounded fellowship of God's children doesn't just "happen" in an unreached area or even in your neighbourhood. When we speak the Truth, we need to have the confidence that it is still the same Truth when it gets through our hearer's language, culture and worldview grid.

The *Cross-Cultural Essentials* curriculum, made up of 10 individual modules, forms a comprehensive training course. Its main goal is to help equip believers to be effective in providing people access to God's Truth through evangelism and discipleship. The *Cross-Cultural Essentials* curriculum makes it easy to be better equipped for teaching the whole narrative of the Bible, for learning about culture and worldview and for planting a church and seeing it grow.

More information on the curriculum can be found at *accesstruth.com*

Introduction to Module 6: Culture & Language Acquisition

The key elements that make up every person's worldview are explored in the beginning of *Culture and Language Acquisition*, helping participants to evaluate and understand the foundations of their own worldview. Several cultures are used as examples to see how different areas of culture can come together to give a cohesive picture. Guidance and advice is given in the area of adjusting to a new culture. Module 6 then covers a practical guide for culture and language acquisition – Becoming Equipped to Communicate – participants are given the handbook and are guided through a series of real-life exercises in their own community to give them an understanding of language and culture learning.

How to use this module

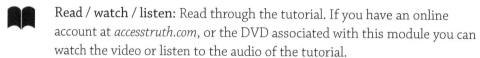 **Read / watch / listen:** Read through the tutorial. If you have an online account at *accesstruth.com*, or the DVD associated with this module you can watch the video or listen to the audio of the tutorial.

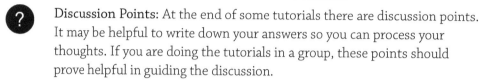 **Discussion Points:** At the end of some tutorials there are discussion points. It may be helpful to write down your answers so you can process your thoughts. If you are doing the tutorials in a group, these points should prove helpful in guiding the discussion.

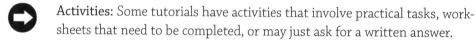 **Activities:** Some tutorials have activities that involve practical tasks, worksheets that need to be completed, or may just ask for a written answer.

Primary Contributors

Paul and Linda Mac

Paul Mac and his wife, Linda, spent 11 years in Papua New Guinea involved in pioneering church planting in an isolated people group. They were privileged to see God plant a number of churches in that area that continue to thrive today. During the time there, they headed up a translation team that produced a New Testament in the local language. After leaving PNG, Paul and Linda worked for 12 years in leadership and consultative roles with an international mission agency. Today they continue to provide church planting guidance for a number of different teams engaged in some of the world's most challenging contexts. They are passionate about seeing churches planted that are well equipped to carry on for future generations.

6.1 Worldviews 1

OBJECTIVES OF THIS TUTORIAL

This is the first of four tutorials exploring the concept of worldview. In this tutorial, we introduce and define the concept of worldview. We look at how all human beings have, and express, a worldview and talk about the concept of meta-narratives.

The notes were transcribed from a video presentation, so watch the video as you read the notes.

Introduction

In this set of materials we are going to be specifically thinking about the concept of "worldview". We want to give an introduction to worldview as a concept because it is very important for us, as we evaluate life for ourselves, and also as we try to grapple with the meaning of life and the ways that other people in other kinds of cultures and situations evaluate life for themselves. So, we are going to reference the idea of worldview back to the notion of *God's Story* - because He is the one who describes the essence of our world for us, and that's what we, as Christian Theists, believe. So we are going to talk about how worldview relates to God's Story.

There is a lot of material to cover in this discussion of worldview, but we would like to give an introduction. We are going to think about the fact that as God's Story is given, other worldviews are formed by human beings - lots of people in this world don't believe God's Story - so how are their worldviews being formed? Why are they being formed? What are they based upon?

We will describe and define what worldview actually is - we will give a definition and talk about what worldview is. That definition will come from others who are thinking and writing about these things - we aren't the only ones thinking and writing about worldview, and we will rely on some other resources that will help us to think about worldview. We will look at some specific examples of worldviews and describe some of the primary features of those.

There are a lot of shades and varieties of worldview. We know that there are 7 billion people in our world today, or more, and if you were to ask each of those individuals to tell you their story - or to give their account of the world to you - their stories would each be different in various ways. So, we are not trying to suggest that we can reduce everyone's view down to eight categories... or ten categories... or twelve categories. We are not trying to be that simplistic. But, we do want to suggest that we can conclude upon a set of categories that tends to cover the majority of the ways that people handle, and think about, the meaning of their lives and their existences. So we will present a number of examples of worldviews and describe some of the core features of them.

We also want to give a picture of a worldview model, or framework, that will help us to understand how to visually encapsulate the idea of worldview - a way that fits with our goals and objectives for the program.

Also, we would like to have enough information to think about and evaluate the worldviews around us. We believe that the best starting point for doing that, is to be able to evaluate our own worldviews first - to be able to critically reflect on what worldview assumptions we actually hold to, and how those are played out in our lives and in our behaviour. So, we need to critically reflect on what our worldview assumptions are, and then we want to be able to apply that critical reflection to others in the world around us as well.

We would also like to consider what it is that motivates worldview change. We are very interested in that concept, because we as Christian Theists - and as people who talk about seeing others evaluate their worldviews and come to understand God's plan and His Story, and who God is, and what He wants them to know about His view of things, and to know Him as the definition of reality - we are going to need to understand about worldview change. We want to see change, so it is a really important concept for us, and we want to understand what God intends in the process of worldview change, and what it is going to take for worldview to shift in that way.

So that is the direction we will be heading in this set of four tutorials on worldview.

Considering our human existence

I have a picture here of a sculpture by Rodin, made in 1902, called "The Thinker". It is a portrait of a person sitting on a stump or a rock, with his elbow on his knee and his fist under his chin. When we as human beings see that portrait, we relate to that picture - we look at a person who is being described in the pose of 'a thinker' - and we say, yes, we understand that picture of a human being considering or thinking through - contemplating - aspects of life and existence, contemplating aspects of meaning in life. That is something that we human beings very closely relate to.

One of the underlying or foundational questions that we ask in the discussion of world-view is - *Why do we pursue an understanding of meaning?*

Around the world, human beings grapple with a common set of issues - a very similar set of questions - about the meaning and the nature of existence. The questions come up time, and time, and time, again. If you go from one culture to another, to another, to another, and you try to understand the way each group of people interpret reality, you begin to see that they are grappling with some very basic questions about the meaning of existence and the meaning of life. We are going to try to grapple with some of those questions and try to describe what some of those common questions are.

We looked at the picture of "The Thinker", now let's look at another picture: of a chimpanzee, or orangutan, who is sitting in a pose, with his legs crossed, his hands folded and his hand under his chin as well. I showed these pictures to my young children, and when they saw the picture of the statue of *The Thinker*, it didn't get much of a response from them, apart from relating to the fact that it is a human being, thinking. But when they see this picture of this chimpanzee or orangutan looking like he is contemplating - with his chin on his hand and looking forward - they chuckle at that, and we do too. We chuckle at the idea that a chimpanzee strikes a similar pose to a human being as a thinker.

For Naturalists - those who believe in the material world only, and no transcendent presence (in other words no one speaking into the material box in which we as human beings live) - that chimpanzee with his chin in his hand looking like he is thinking, is a person in the process of becoming a self conscious thinker. But we instinctively as human beings, know that, when we see those two pictures, we are not describing the same thing. We have to have a certain presupposition - we have to presume something - in order to even contemplate the idea of *thinking* about worldview. Because we have to explain or describe the difference between the chimpanzee - with his chin in his hands supposedly thinking - and the human being, who is a legitimate thinker, contemplating existence.

In some worldviews, their starting point for answering the very basic question - *What is the difference between a thinking human being contemplating the meaning of life and a chimpanzee who looks like he is contemplating?* - is very different. It is very difficult for some worldviews to answer that question, because the presuppositions underpinning their worldviews don't provide a substantial basis for resolving that very question: about the act or ability that human beings have to contemplate the difference in their life vs. the life of an animal.

We do have some thoughts about that as Christians. Those are the things we would like to describe or at least introduce in greater detail, so that we can begin thinking about them for ourselves.

All human beings have a worldview

There is a natural tendency that human beings have, to deal 'worldviewishly'; to think and live in worldview terms.

We are going to look at the painting (*The Gulf Stream by Winslow Homer: 1890s*). When we express ourselves artistically or creatively we tend to demonstrate our 'inner working' or our core commitments. In the painting, Winslow Homer has depicted an ocean scene (the Gulf Stream was something he was very familiar with) and we can see a number of objects in that painting that catch our attention. There are five or six objects that capture the nature of this painting for us.

The first thing we can see - because it is front and centre - is a broken-down, relatively small, boat with its mast broken and seemingly drifting with the sea around it. The sea is not calm, and as you look at it you notice that in the water in the forefront you see quite a number of sharks that don't look particularly friendly either. There is a tinge of red in a number of places in the water, which would at least give the impression of blood in the water. The man who is in the boat is not well dressed; he only has on a pair of pants. He is also a black person, and at that time and era in American life, that kind of individual would not have had a great standing in society. Then as we look in the background - in the right hand corner - we see a waterspout, which is not a welcome sight for people on the ocean, because it has a lot of destructive power. Then way up in the left hand corner, on the horizon, as you look closely at the painting, in the clouds and the shading of the clouds, you can see the masts of a ship - very faintly in the distance.

As we look at this picture, we see a grim picture; we don't see a happy picture there. The point isn't to over-evaluate the painting, as an art critic might. But the point is this: we, as human beings, are also artistic and creative beings. As Christian Theists we would say we are creative beings because God Himself is creative and that is part of His identity. We as creative beings *exude* worldview. In this painting, Winslow Homer is portraying a very grim worldview - but even though it is grim, we can see that he is portraying *something*. When critics look at this painting they see a portrayal of the world around us as a very difficult place - that we are on a boat that is taking us in a direction that we are not clear about, that there are a lot of obstacles in the world, there are a lot of dangers and a lot of ways in which our lives may not end up positively.

So, as we evaluate this kind of human creative process - as we read, as we watch movies - we see artistic expression *demonstrating* core commitments of worldview. That is a natural occurrence for human beings. Human beings do that by definition - time and time and time again that occurs. One of the questions we are asking is, *Why*? Another question we are asking is, *What*? What is actually demonstrated in artistic and other forms of expression that point back to worldview commitments?

Worldview is something that we as human beings *do* or that we *hold to*, that helps us to explain the meaning of our existence. Worldviews are a description of meaning in relationship to our existence as human beings.

Two worldview resources

Two worldview resources that we will be referring to during these four tutorials are:

James W. Sire. *The Universe Next Door: A Basic Worldview Catalog*, 5th Edition. Kindle Edition. 2009.

Steve Wilkens & Mark L. Sanford. *Hidden Worldviews: Eight Cultural Stories That Shape Our Lives*. Kindle Edition. 2009.

James Sire is a Christian philosopher and apologist, and in his book he describes worldview in a theoretical, formally descriptive way. He does that deliberately to contrast other worldview systems with the worldview system of Christian Theism. He includes in his book, a description of traditional religious worldview systems. He gives a definition of 'worldview' and then he outlines a set of *universal questions* that we can ask to arrive at a description of any given worldview. We can use these universal questions to help us to understand where another worldview stands, in what Sire considers to be some critical areas. Then Sire explains some of the strengths and weaknesses of these worldviews - how they stand up - in comparison to Christian Theism. We will be looking at some of these universal questions later in these tutorials because they are helpful in explaining or describing worldview systems.

The second book - by Wilkens and Sanford - takes a less formal approach. They are trying to describe worldviews that they describe as being *lived worldviews*. They don't go into comparing religious worldviews - such as comparing Islam and Christianity - because they are describing the more subtle influences of cultural shaping in our lives. They look at the kinds of influences in our societies and cultures that tend to come in and shape the ways that we think and live. They are deliberately taking a less formal approach, but are describing some very pertinent areas of worldview and worldview formation for us, and they are describing it from the perspective of the *story* that each of us lives - the story that undergirds and supports our life and that our worldview derives from. That is a good concept for us because it relates to some of the things we think and talk about in terms of God's Story and God's relationship to us in our story.

Hopefully you will have an opportunity to look at these two books yourself. We will be referring to them in the next three tutorials as we move ahead, but not covering them exhaustively. It would be good for you to look at them yourself.

A Definition of Worldview

The following definition is from James Sire, but it is the same definition that is used by the authors of the other book as well.

> Worldview is a commitment, a fundamental orientation of the heart, that can be expressed as a story or in a set of presuppositions (assumptions which may be true, partially true or entirely false) that we hold (consciously or subconsciously, consistently or inconsistently) about the basic constitution of reality, and that provides the foundation on which we live and move and have our being. (Sire)

Meta-narrative

Before we look at this definition in more detail, there is a need to look at the concept of *meta-narrative*. So, what is a meta-narrative? If you talk about meta-narrative in our post-modern world today - the Western world - you will run into a great deal of skepticism about the notion of meta-narrative. But we think of a meta-narrative as an overarching story that people believe in - usually a group of people - that ties reality together for them, that fundamentally joins together the aspects of reality for them. We believe that worldviews are meta-narratives - those commitments that we make at a heart level are overarching stories to tie reality together for us.

Historically, we have seen a steady movement away from a belief in the explanatory power of meta-narratives. Pre-modernists were very religious and very skeptical of scientific knowledge. Then we moved into a period of modernism where there was an explosion of industry, and understanding and science and an amazing growing awareness of the intricate nature of God's creation, and a growing belief that science could provide answers for life. Then there was an increasing skepticism about science's ability to provide answers and a movement toward Post-modernism, which is a belief in a

relative view of truth - that there is no meta-narrative that describes and holds reality together for us. So, there has been a shift from concrete belief in religious, or spiritual concepts, to a belief in science or naturalism, to a skepticism about either being able to provide a meta-narrative that describes reality.

So we will run into people today who are extremely skeptical about meta-narratives. In worldview terms we can describe even that position of skepticism as a meta-narrative - that is a vicious cycle that some post-modern thinkers find themselves in.

Our story and God's Story

Worldviews are fundamental orientations of our hearts. The Biblical concept of 'the heart' takes in the human person as a whole. These orientations of our hearts - these commitments - can be expressed as stories, and we as human beings have stories - each of us has a story. Our stories are the way that our worldview unfolds. If I was to describe my entire life story to you, you would be able to look at my story and find that my story gives you a good understanding of what my meta-narrative process or my worldview process has been about. You would find the elements of my worldview in my story.

This orientation of our hearts is based on a story, and often if worldviews are formalised, those stories can be defined as a set of presuppositions - these assumptions that are summary statements of the core commitments that I have made. About who God is, about God and His nature - I believe in a triune, personal, transcendent God who has created all things and has love and care for all the things that He has created, and has a personal relationship with what He has created. That is a presupposition that I would be operating on the basis of, as a Christian Theist.

Those presuppositions are almost always derived from a story. My story is connected to another overarching story, which is God's. Some of us hold to our commitments more or less consistently. Sometimes we are not aware of our commitments on that level. Sometimes we hold to things that we don't understand clearly, in our conscious self, but we find that, "Oh, yeah, I have bought into that." I have bought into that presupposition about life, even though I wasn't aware of it. That happens to us as believers, and is something we have to be on guard against, which is a concept that Wilkens and Sanford particularly focus on.

So, these presuppositions that we hold to are sometimes consistent and sometimes inconsistent. But they provide information for us about the basic constitution of our world, of our reality. They help us to understand reality, and they are the foundation for what we do.

As we think of worldviews as a story, we know that our worldviews are not static. They are in flux (not necessarily our core commitments, although core commitments can, and do change). Our worldviews change as our stories move forward.

My son's worldview - at eight or ten years old - may be founded on some of the same presuppositions that I hold to as a Christian Theist, but obviously there is a lot of

changing, growing and expanding that will occur in the course of his story. My story today is not the same as it was ten years ago. I, as a maturing and changing person, see change in my worldview. Our stories are changing, growing and expanding - which makes worldviews messy, but we can describe a set of presuppositions that we hold to at a heart level that provide a foundation for our reality.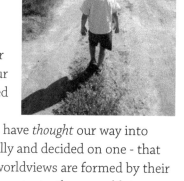

Worldviews can also be described as being *absorbed* rather than *adopted*. We see worldviews being absorbed from our nature and from our nurture - we absorb what is described and defined from our social environments and from our physical environments. It is not as if we as human beings have *thought* our way into worldviews; that we have compared all the systems logically and decided on one - that is not how worldview formation works for people. Their worldviews are formed by their social and physical circumstances. In many of the world's contexts, those worldviews are not formally defined the way that we are talking about worldview today; they are generated in bits and pieces. We will look more at these ideas in the next tutorial, as well as some specific questions to help guide us in identifying and evaluating worldviews.

⦿ DISCUSSION POINTS

1. How has your worldview changed since you were a child?

2. What specific influences can you pinpoint that caused the most significant changes in your worldview?

➡ ACTIVITIES

1. Look at the artworks below - all by the same artist - and write a few points about what you think they might express about the worldview of the artist.

2. Now do a little research to find out more about the creator of the artworks above - British sculptor Andy Goldsworthy (born 26 July 1956). Find out anything about his worldview, what he values, etc. and see if he did express those things to you through his artwork.

Worldviews 2

OBJECTIVES OF THIS TUTORIAL

This is the second tutorial on the area of worldview. We will look at a model that helps us to understand the nature of a person's worldview, and at eight questions that help us to investigate and understand other worldviews around us.
The notes were transcribed from a video presentation, so watch the video as you read the notes.

Last Time

In our first tutorial on worldview:

- we tried to begin to describe and define what worldviews are and where they come from
- we gave a definition of worldview - from James Sire
- we also mentioned another resource from Wilkens and Sanford
- we talked about meta-narratives, the overarching stories that tie reality together for us
- we described God's meta-narrative - in the sense that God has a major Story, and that He wants us to understand what that Story is and He wants us to be a part of that
- we talked about the human heart and the fact that humans are motivated to be 'worldviewish' - we are motivated to live according to a set of presuppositions that ultimately drives our behaviour
- we described the informality of worldview formation and the fact that our worldview is changing, growing and expanding - that our own personal stories have worldview issues attached to them - our experience accumulates and is added to our worldview as part of an informal process of worldview formation. This happens in Western societies and also in minority societies around the world where worldview is also an underpinning of society and of culture.

Identifying worldviews

We are going to move on to a series of questions by James Sire, that are based on the definition of worldview, and that Sire describes as being able to help us to identify the formal worldview that is in place in a given situation.

We are not saying that we would go into a setting and ask these worldview questions and therefore discern people's worldviews, by going in to a situation and saying, 'I have eight questions for you. Can you answer these questions then I'll know everything about you, I'll have you nicely pigeon-holed and we can move on, so I'll know how to approach you from here on out'. No, that's not the point. But the point is that as we get to know the stories of others, these questions provide an underlying framework for us to identify and evaluate life commitments.

A worldview model

So, we want to know what the answers to these questions are, but before that we will look at a model of worldview that you may have seen before which is a diagram with concentric circles that move toward a centre (see diagram below). We want to know how to identify someone's worldview (and we are going to talk about those questions from Sire) so, what kind of a conceptual model helps us to do that?

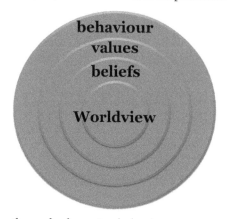

If you look at the diagram, it starts on the outermost circle with *behaviour*. Why behaviour? The simple answer is, why not behaviour?

When we see a person we see behaviour, first and foremost. Even if we don't know the language that a person is speaking, we can begin to see and understand them through their behaviour. When I go to a society overseas and go through the 'meet and greet' process (before I know the local language), it helps me to understand hospitality in that setting. Very quickly, through observing behaviour, we get an idea of the system of belief that underpins that society.

To understand how to interpret behaviour, we have to go further than that, we need to actually understand the *values* that are motivating behaviour. Sometimes the outcomes of behaviour are very different, but there is a set of values - in certain cases that surprises us - that underpins behaviour. In most cases we see the consistent threads there. So values are those things that we are committed to living out through our behaviour that we would describe by saying, 'Yes, I highly value this, therefore I act in a certain way'.

So, in our set of concentric circles, we are moving toward commitments that are more and more key to us. That is the idea in this model. So we start with the observable - the behaviour. Then we describe values in the second circle, then we move to the things that we would call *beliefs*. These move back away from practical outworking towards core commitments or presuppositions that underpin what we do in this world or how we think in this world.

Human beings seek to make sense of reality

Human beings are 'hard wired' to make sense of their reality - of the world around them - in some way or other - even if they conclude that there is no way to make sense of it. They are still making a statement that 'You can't make sense of it, it doesn't have any sense, it is chaos.' That in itself is a description of the nonsense of the attempt to make sense. So *everyone* is working in this direction - they have behaviour, they have values, they have beliefs about things. Those beliefs direct and steer their values - the lower level of the set of assumptions that they are operating from - and then in this model, at the centre is *worldview* itself.

Worldview is at the centre because it is the most firmly held commitments that I make - the things that I will not give up, that I will not compromise on in my intellectual being. Those are the things that I hold very tightly to and that I will be very strong in defending. Sometimes, as Sire points out, those things are not *consciously* held, so it is a bit difficult to defend something that you have not tangibly pinned down. But, for those of us who adhere to religious worldviews that are fairly well defined - like Christian Theism - most of those commitments we can articulate in some way or other and we understand why we are committed to those things.

As we said, human beings are hard wired to make this kind of sense of reality, even those who reject the notion that we are trying to make sense... are trying to make sense. So, it is very difficult to get away from making sense of reality, from trying to define and describe the *Why* of what is in the 'box' of our reality. It is very, very difficult - and I would say *impossible* - for rational human beings to disconnect themselves from trying to make meaning of this reality that we deal with all the time. This is a God-given ability; a deliberate statement about what God has done in creating human beings.

A problem with the model

There is a problem with this particular worldview model that we should mention. We define *worldview* at the core or at the centre of the diagram (and although this isn't Sire's model, he would have a similar perspective to this also). If you describe worldview as a set of *intellectual* commitments and not *heart* commitments, then a disconnect can be allowed between what we say is our worldview, and what we see in our behaviour.

We can think of an example of religiously oriented people, such as the idea of a 'non-practising Jew', or a 'non-practising Muslim' or a 'non-practising Hindu'. When I hear someone describe someone else as a 'non-practising Christian', that, to me, is an oxymoron (it is self-contradictory) and you would probably say the same thing. Christians, by definition, are *practicing*. Why? Because the hub of our worldview as a Christian Theist will motivate our beliefs, values and behaviours in such a way that it is not possible to be a non-practising adherent of true Christianity. We would say that.

Now, there are lots of stages of people growing as Christians, who don't understand the whole picture of what our identity with Christ is all about - I don't - but I am growing in my understanding of what my identity in Christ is about and what that implies for me as God sees me in Christ, what that means for the outworking of my beliefs, values and behaviours. So, as I grow in understanding, internalising and applying that, then the worldview commitments that I have made become sharper. The presuppositions themselves, I believe, become sharper, but also my life on a worldview level cannot disengage from my behaviour. It necessarily connects outward toward my behaviour.

So, one of the problems with this model is the allowance of a disconnect between core commitments and behaviour - so somebody can act like a pagan behaviourally and still claim to hold to a set of intellectual commitments that they would define as 'Christian'. Obviously the argument can be made that they don't really hold to those commitments.

So, when we separate out worldview and put it at the centre as if it doesn't also encapsulate our behaviour - that the whole configuration isn't in itself worldview - when we describe worldview in the center as a set of commitments and then describe beliefs, values and behaviours as *other* things, that aren't worldview itself - it creates an unhelpful separation between all the areas and facets of our life. Human beings are whole beings - God made them that way - and that's why Sire made adjustments to his definition about commitments being *heart* commitments that are *lived*.

Eight Questions

There are eight questions that Sire lists to help us to identify worldview commitments:

1. *What defines reality?*
2. *What is the nature of external reality, that is, the world around us?*
3. *What is a human being?*
4. *What happens to a person at death?*
5. *Why is it possible to know anything at all?*
6. *How do we know what is right and wrong?*
7. *What is the meaning of human history?*
8. *What personal, life-orienting core commitments are consistent with this worldview?*

1. What defines reality?

His first question has to do with an area of philosophy called 'metaphysics'. Metaphysics is 'the nature of reality', or what *defines* reality for us. What is the starting point of reality - what is *really real* in our lives?

There are a lot of answers that are given to this question, depending on the worldview that the person ascribes to. For us as Christian Theists, we say our origin point for reality is God Himself: that God exists, He is a certain kind of being, He has a certain kind of identity, He is described, explained, in a certain Story, and that Story and His identity provide the basis for our understanding of reality. God Himself is reality. God Himself defines what reality means. God Himself defines the fact that we as human beings look for meaning, because He is a meaning-maker, He builds meaning, He is the One who creates, He is the One who is creative, therefore we are creative, He is rational, therefore we are rational, etc. etc.

The definition of reality is a critical issue in describing worldview because a Naturalist, for example, describes reality in terms of the material world. For them the material world *is* reality - the origin point for reality is the eternality of matter. What we are going to be moving toward in the next tutorials is the idea that defining reality *without* a transcendent being involved - someone speaking into the 'box' from outside - doesn't allow us to reasonably live life in a consistent way.

For our purpose now, the range of answers we get when asking that question, allows us to get a sense of where a worldview is headed. Our origin point for reality is God Himself, the origin point of reality for a Naturalist is matter, or the material world. We call this the person's metaphysical position - what do they believe about the nature of reality? What is really real?

2. What is the nature of external reality, that is, the world around us?

As you can imagine, these dots all connect - our origin point for reality points us toward an explanation of the nature of external reality. If reality originates with God, then *external* reality originated with God, and has a certain kind of order (or lack thereof) based on who God Himself is. That is what we as Christians describe.

So, when we talk about reality, we talk about God: His character. One of His character traits is that He is all-powerful, another that He is all-knowing, another that He is Omnipresent: that He is everywhere. So, as we apply His character traits: His goodness, His love, His transcendence, His Truth-giving nature, His communicative nature, to external reality, we begin to see His character traits and apply them to the world. We talk about the world as a description of who His Being is - His *ontological* nature. God, as the reference point for the nature of being, helps to give us an explanation of external reality.

Those who are Naturalists would say that external reality is just chaos. It follows 'natural laws', but ultimately it is chaos, it is matter moving forward, but not particularly in any direction (which is a topic we will delve into later), there is no 'end goal' process for nature for a naturalist. It is just moving according to a set of natural laws that themselves have somehow evolved, because of certain kinds of characteristics. There is no overarching causality to that system and that creates a dilemma for the Naturalist.

3. What is a human being?

This is a complicated question, and has to do with *ontology* (the nature of being). It is a complicated question for those who don't have a transcendent voice speaking into our matter - our 'box' - because that view requires that human beings are highly complicated, evolved machines (for a Naturalist for example).

For us as believers, we have started with the origin point of reality as God Himself - His nature and His character, His work - therefore a human being for us is a person made in God's image and bearing the stamp of God Himself in a number of ways. That helps us to explain the very person that is 'human'. That helps us, when we look at the picture of 'the Thinker' and the monkey, to know that the line of division has to do with the image of God. For a Naturalist, that line of division is not in place, because (to them) there is no person made in the image of God, as something separate from an ape.

There are a lot of worldview definitions of human beings - in the New Age philosophy they extend evolution to go into psychic ability and other kinds of evolution that are still ongoing for us as human beings, that when we fully realize those we will just be astonished at how little we know today, intellectually, psychically, spiritually, etc. There are all kinds of definitions, but we need to know what people think about what constitutes human nature and human make-up.

4. What happens to a person at death?

This is a question very much asked these days around the world, and in every era, really. What is it that happens to a person at death? Do persons simply cease to exist - are their beings extinguished? If you are a Naturalist, you have to conclude that the complex machine that existed, when it dies, it stops existing and becomes part of the material universe in the same way it was a part of the material universe before it lived. So there is no transformation to a higher state, there is no reincarnation or departure to the 'other side'.

For Christian Theists, of course, we see this natural world as leading us to a place of God's Kingdom, God's Heaven (either that, or the reality of Hell). So, we give answers to the question in very different ways than many worldviews do. People around the world are asking this question and they do have complex answers that they are giving for that question. It is not that the category exists just for Christians and selected others; it is remarkable that concepts of eternal reward or eternal punishment come into play all over the world. Before the Yanamamo people ever heard about a transcendent God, they had a concept of eternal reward and eternal punishment. We also hear this about some of the Indians who lived in the Americas in the early years before European involvement - they believed in eternal places and destinies. People around the world also believe that spiritual beings from the dead also exist and that they affect others. The idea of 'spiritual life' and 'spirituality' after death is certainly not a new concept and it is a very common concept that we grapple with as we investigate people's worldviews.

5. Why is it possible to know anything at all?

This question is based on the other questions we have asked, and it has to do with an area of philosophy called *epistemology*. Epistemology is about knowledge - being able to know. Why is it possible to know anything at all? Why are we aware, why are we knowledgeable at all?

We as believers say we have self-awareness, or are rational and able to communicate because we have been created in the image of an all-knowing God who has those characteristics, who has that nature. That is a fairly simple answer for us, as we connect the dots back to the question that we started with, which is God defining reality. But, for a Naturalist - a person who doesn't believe in any transcendent being, and that matter is all that there is, and who describes the developmental process of life in terms of causality and chance with no end goal in mind - it is a very complex question. It is a very difficult question - at what point does the transition occur from the monkey to the man? When does a man develop consciousness? There is obvious instinctive action from the monkey, there is apparent conscious action from the man (although some Naturalists believe that action is somehow *determined* and is not a conscious choice).

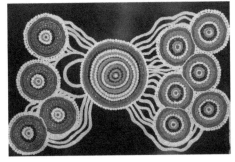

Pathways to knowledge -
Aboriginal artist Denise Proud, 2011

Worldviews have to have some sort of an explanation for epistemology - the fact that we can know anything at all. Worldviews around the world that are folk worldviews think less formally about this issue than we do, but it is still an important question to ask nonetheless, because it points us back to the question of; "Who is telling the Truth - who can give access to knowledge - who provides knowledge to mankind?" That is a very important question that goes back step-by-step to the definition of reality - for us, defined by God Himself as the provider of truth and knowledge.

6. How do we know what is right and wrong?

As a logical outcome of us concluding that God created, and that He created man in His image, He gave man a concept of right and wrong. We say that because it is a logical outcome of who God is - what His character is about - His goodness to give man an understanding of the knowledge of right and wrong. He is the Truth-giver.

For those who work in other kinds of systems, this question is complicated - how do we know what is right and wrong? Is it just about our human choices, making a consistent set of choices or about what is defined as right and wrong in our particular culture or social environments? Are there universal rights and wrongs? It is very hard for someone who doesn't start with Theism to actually believe that there are defined and absolute rights and wrongs - and in fact we see that in our world all around us today, that Postmodernists are very sceptical about the notion of right and wrong.

Other societies around the world have obvious things that are 'right' and things that are 'wrong', and we desire to know why that is the case. How do you as a society know what things are right and what things are wrong? And we want to know if those views that are expressed are consistently acted upon. Are people consistently making those choices according to what they *say* their presupposition is about how we know what is right and what is wrong? That is an important question to ask in understanding worldviews.

7. What is the meaning of human history?

This is important because in a Naturalistic system, for example, the meaning of human history is that there is no meaning to human history. There is no ultimate goal or purpose to the run of history in Naturalism - it is just evolving and happening, there is causation through natural laws and processes, but there is no ultimate goal to human history. That is very depressing to us.

We believe that God Himself originated history - it is His Story - and He has some plans and goals in mind for that. We can trust in His goals and His plans in relation to human history, and we spend a lot of our time explaining God's purposes for this world and for life and for history. He is the One who is the origin point for time and issues related to history.

Those are two very different outcomes for the question about human history. In other societies around the world, human history is often defined cyclically - it happens in cycles of time or history - that history is not as linear as it is for us in the Western world or as Christian Theists view history. So, there are a lot of different answers to that question.

8. What personal, life-orienting core commitments are consistent with this

worldview?

This is a question that Sire added to his original set of seven questions, because of the problem we noted earlier. When we look at the worldview-centred model, working outward toward behaviour, we can, if we are not careful, see a disconnect.

When we evaluate the answers to the first seven questions, do we see that the personal life-orienting core commitments are derived from those answers or not? A Christian Theist has no difficulty - if they live in accordance with the core commitments described in God's Story - in explaining how those core commitments are an outworking of the answers to those seven questions. However, for many of the worldviews around us, it is quite difficult to answer those questions, for example from a Naturalistic point of view (cause-free, transcendent-free, only matter in the box) and to describe how and why they live a certain kind of way as a result of the answers to those questions. There are no 'connect-the-dots' links, and you close the box off to how and why you live a certain way as a result. That is a very complicated issue for many of these worldviews, as we will continue to see as we move forward.

So, this set of questions can help us to think about worldviews, and help us to describe the worldviews that we encounter as we look around the world and look inside of our own societies today.

 DISCUSSION POINTS

1. Australia was once, but is no longer considered a Christian country. What behaviours in our society point to the fact that values, beliefs and worldview in general have changed from being based on a Christian Theist worldview?

2. Do you notice any ways in which the prevailing worldview comes into direct conflict with your own Biblical worldview - in terms of making your behaviour different from those in the wider community?

➡ ACTIVITIES

1. Over the course of the next weeks, find one or more people you know well, and have a discussion with them based on the first seven of Sire's questions. Try to talk to people with a perspective other than a Christian Theist worldview if you can. During your discussion think about how their worldview ties together, if they have thought about these questions very much before (and why or why not) and if they seem convinced and sure of their position or not.

6.3 Worldviews 3

OBJECTIVES OF THIS TUTORIAL

This tutorial builds on our worldview definition, and looks further at some weaknesses in common, non-theistic, worldviews. We will also describe some characteristics of the most common worldviews that people hold.

The notes were transcribed from a video presentation, so watch the video as you read the notes.

Introduction

As we look at some of the common worldviews in the world today, we will be asking some of the questions that James Sire outlined in his book. Sire actually goes through each of these worldviews and applies his eight questions to each one. We are not going to take the discussion to that depth, but we will simply present an overview of each of the worldviews he lists, and allow each of you to read those books (mentioned in tutorial 6.1) at your leisure.

These issues are very significant for us, as we try to apply the study of worldview to other cultures and other places around the world. It will help us to have an understanding of the basic kinds of questions and presuppositions that they will be operating from, and what better place to begin than with our own worldviews? Lots of these worldviews that we will be discussing in the next two tutorials come from a secular perspective and a Western perspective.

In Sire's list, he describes the worldviews according to the progression of thought in philosophical development - the progression of Western societal thought. He describes a fairly clear picture of how the philosophy of life and the meaning of life moved gradually away from a description centred in the person of God, and in the reality of God. It moved toward bases that are more scientific and we see an undermining of *meaning* - the ability of human beings to feel, to sense, to describe meaning - and a consequent move away from trustworthy sources for truth. We will describe that in greater detail as we talk about these worldview systems.

Our own worldview - Christian Theism

We will begin by mentioning our own worldview, which is Christian Theism. Christian Theism looks at these eight questions that Sire has given in a very specific way. It goes back to the reality of God - the metaphysical fact of God's existence - the definition or reality in the person of God. Who God is, what His character is, what He has done; what His acts have been about and how His reality defines the external reality for us - the things we see around us.

His story provides a narrative framework for us. He defines our reality. He defines what human beings are. He defines what happens to a person after death. Because of human beings being made in His image, they are eternal beings, like He is. He is a Spirit, but we are eternal beings with bodies and souls, and our souls are an eternal aspect of who we are.

He defines right and wrong for us, He defines the existence of evil and the reason for the existence of evil. He defines how we have knowledge, what the category of knowledge - the epistemological category - is for us as human beings; God defines that. He defines what we believe in terms of our core commitments. In other words: as our beliefs and values are  working their way out toward our behaviour - what motivates our core commitments and the outworking of those commitments practically, what motivates and drives our actual behaviour: He defines those things on the basis of who He is.

So, Christian Theism is a system in which all of the primary questions - all of the major questions and categories of life - are answered. And, they are answered in what we believe to be a coherent and consistent fashion. We don't leave out big pieces of life and say 'At this time we can't answer the question of meaning, or the question of truth, or the question of right and wrong, or the question of death and life'. We can, and do, answer those questions, like the nature of human beings.

So, that is a description of Christian Theism. Now, as we move forward in time, we begin to see, in the period after the Middle Ages, after the dark time of human existence for many, that a growing confidence was emerging in science and the ability of science to progress and to solve life's dilemmas. 'If we could only have scientific achievement maximised, the human dilemma and the problem of pain and suffering, those issues would be resolved' - that was some of the belief that motivated the system that emerged second, which we will talk about now, Deism.

Deism

Deism is a belief that although God Himself was present in the creation of the system in which we live - the 'box' in which we live - that He functioned more like the metaphor of a 'clockmaker'. So that He instituted the processes that we observe in the world around us - naturalistic processes - and as our clockmaker He 'wound up' the universe and now He is allowing that universe to proceed forward in the fashion that it does according to the natural laws that He instituted, according to a set of causality processes that He Himself instituted. But, in effect, He is not present to give oversight on a regular basis to this universe. God has removed Himself from the scene and in practical terms He does not have input into the system. The system is closed - to what exists in material terms.

For a Deist then, practically or pragmatically they function as Naturalists. So, as Deism moved forward, the reliance on or the need for God became less and less significant. So, a natural progression then from Deism then is the third worldview that Sire describes, which is Naturalism.

Naturalism

Naturalism has stopped talking about the 'clockmaker' who initiated a process, and now is just describing what is in the 'box'. When we say what is in the box, we are talking about what we can observe and handle - what is tangible to our senses. We are talking about the material world, and any of the answers that we give as to ultimate reality and the outworking of ultimate reality, can only go back to a material universe. They can't begin any other place. That has some major implications for the answers to the other of Sire's questions - for whether or not there is a soul, or a part of a human being that survives death. Most likely the answer would be 'No', in a naturalistic system. There is no 'soul stuff' in the true sense of non-material entity. There is no rationality or there is no image-of-God humanness, there is no ultimate truth claims made by Naturalism except those which derive from natural processes and nature itself.

There are no 'rights' and 'wrongs' that are transcendent truth - that speak into the closed system - because the system is indeed closed to absolute judgements about truth and right and wrong. So, for Naturalists then, the answers to the questions are very much shaped by their presuppositional starting point which is the material world around them.

As Naturalism developed as a system, scepticism was growing about the ability of Naturalists to answer the fundamental questions about the meaning of life. Scepticism was in fact growing about the notion that meaning existed at all in a naturalistic environment. Bear in mind that Naturalists (and we are generalising here, because there are shades and varieties in all these worldviews) would conclude that the mechanistic processes by which we live and breathe are *determined* - they are not changing - they are eternal processes and laws. In the same way that a lion does not sit and contemplate whether or not it will attack a zebra today because that might be considered murder. When a lion has opportunity to kill a zebra, he kills the zebra, because that is their instinct. For a Naturalist, that process also can and often does apply to human beings so that our outcomes are determined - we don't have true choice in the way that we think we do. For many Naturalists, we as human beings do not have a true sense, or ability to choose. That is called *determinism*. Not all Naturalists would fit into that camp, but certainly a number would. As that philosophy of life works its way out, there arose within the Naturalists a group of people that we would call Nihilists.

Nihilism

The Nihilists basically see Naturalism as a process, where the natural outworking is indeed futility. There is no ultimate meaning to life because we are part of a determined machine, part of a mechanistic system governed by laws determined in process and determined in causality. Therefore our lives are essentially futile.

There is a large body of literature that has arisen as a result of this Nihilistic outlook - literature, poetry, movies to some extent - you can find a genre of materials that are devoted to a description of a Nihilistic outlook. Some people trace the atrocities from WW2 and other things back to a Nihilistic outlook. Some of the philosophers that would be strong proponents of Nihilism, some of them ultimately - because of their sense of futility and their lack of ability to find ultimate meaning - either committed suicide or lost their minds.

Nihilism as a system was very much a response to Naturalism and determinism and the lack of any ultimate meaning in Naturalism. Nihilism as a philosophical development pushed people back to a search for meaning - but meaning was only being defined by what was 'in the box', not by something that transcended what was in the box - in other words a 'god-person'.

Existentialism

Then the Existentialists said, 'We can't define meaning. We are Naturalists by 'calling'. We can't define meaning by someone speaking into the box from the outside.' Although there *was* a 'Christian' variety of Existentialism that did arise and was very subjective in nature in terms of God speaking to human beings - so not all Existentialists were Naturalists. But as we look at the process of philosophical development, Existentialism came out of Naturalism, because Existentialists began to describe meaning as being about 'my freedom to choose' - my subjective ability to choose.

So, in secular societies (non-religious societies) *my ability to choose* was my statement of defiance against a Naturalistic and Nihilistic system. If I wanted to have meaning, I had to define that meaning for myself, through my own choices and my own decision-making. Existentialism was an attempt to inject meaning back into a closed system.

That attempt ultimately failed. There is no good or realistic way - without a source of being that stems from the character of a transcendent God - to inject meaning back into a closed system. So, the Existentialists attempted that and they were unsuccessful.

Now we will take a slight detour into looking at another worldview that Sire talks about which is not in the progression that we have been describing, but it has had influence in some Western societies. He (Sire) felt that some comparative religious views should be included, so he describes Eastern Pantheistic Monism.

Eastern Pantheistic Monism

Eastern; from the East, or non-Western. *Pantheism*; the view that essentially *all is God*, that everything that there is, is part of God. Nature is God and the substance of God is found in being around us. So, we as human beings are part of the constitution and definition of God. *Monism;* that all is one.

So, Eastern Pantheistic Monistic systems describe the nature of reality in terms of our growing toward 'oneness' with 'the one'. These systems include things like Buddhism and Hinduism. It is very simplistic for us to try to lump all of those things together because there are many, many varieties and different ways that these things are described, different ways that those who are believers in these systems would explain what they believe. But, Eastern Pantheistic Monism does tend to lump together some common categories and areas of Hinduism and Buddhism and tries to define the ways in which we as human beings are becoming more and more aware, through giving up our own individuality, that we are *one with the one* - with the pantheism that is 'god'. And that our current self-awareness or self-absorption is an illusion for us. So there is this movement toward a monism, or oneness, that is a process for us as human beings. Another area that the West did buy into, as a response to Existentialism, is New Age Thinking.

New Age

New Age is a reaction to the extreme secularism of Naturalism, Nihilism and even Existentialism, and is a move back to trying to find spirituality, but certainly not a move back toward God. A move back toward mystical, and psychic versions of spirituality - astrological versions of spirituality. All of the bizarre (which may seem pejorative to some New Age thinkers...), occultist, peculiar ways to recapture spirituality - even going back to animism, shamanism and drug use - were a part of this attempt to encapsulate 'spirituality' with the barrenness in the life of human beings as a consequence of the deterministic, closed system of Naturalism.

New Age thinking is very eclectic, very hard to encapsulate - it was almost a fad in the 1980s, but it has continued to exist, and we still see some effects of this today. Some famous people from movies and other strong and big personalities are proponents of this sort of view, and so we hear about it and it is good for us to be aware of it. It is a secular spirituality, almost - a spirituality in the absence of God.

New Agers, when they describe human beings and the direction of history, would be describing our developing psychic or supernatural thinking ability - ESP (extra sensory perception) and these kinds of things. Many of them would be describing those things as our move toward enlightenment, and that human evolution as a process is moving toward that kind of enlightenment, that kind awareness, that kind of ability to use psychic powers and extra-sensory powers to control, harness, develop, for finding salvation. All of these systems we have mentioned have some element of salvation to them - we will talk about that later.

So, New Age thinking is a reaction to Existentialism in the West - most of these world-views are Western focused - because that is the world we are all living in. New Age was one kind of reaction to Naturalism, Nihilism and Existentialism, and another is what we think of now as Postmodernism.

Postmodernism

Postmodernism was a strong response to *absolute* claims - a strong response to the fact that religious absolutism, like Christian Theism or some other kinds of Theism, was not adequately solving the problems of life; that Christian claims actually led to a lot of atrocities in war and other problems in Europe and in the West in general; that 'Christians' were not describing a worldview that was detached from pain and suffering, (and we use the term Christian very broadly to include the Roman Catholic church and other institutions which were highly corrupted), but were contributing to and partic-ipating in very distasteful processes of human society. They were contributing to the problem of evil itself: warfare, slavery and other things.

So, Postmodernists are reacting on the one hand to this religiosity that seems like hy-pocrisy, and on the other hand they are reacting to the claims of science which said that science was the salvation methodology that we needed - that if science could solve life's problems we would all be okay. Postmodernists would say that science (and religious systems) gave us as many problems as it solved - pollution, the destruction of our environment, corruption, infighting, competition for resources, religious division, world division, division over ideology, nationalism, and the opportunity to kill each other in more efficient ways. So, Postmodernists would say that in light of the lies and distortions of science and religion, what we are left with is a system in which clearly, objective truth and objective reference points are not possible. Therefore, truth itself is relative to societal influence, and tolerance - our ability to tolerate one another - is what we should live according to. Tolerance is law - it is the way that we should live for Postmodernists.

That is a very common view today. As you 'hear' the society around you, there are threads of Postmodernism in much of it, and Postmodernism creeps into the Church, which is something that we will continue to discuss in our next tutorial.

Islamic Theism

The final worldview that Sire mentions is Islamic Theism. He describes it because he feels that Islamic Theism has a higher profile than it ever has before: with the terrorist issues, the World Trade Centre bombings, and the collective effort from Australia, the US and other countries to target terrorist activity in very specific ways as it is an affront to our ways of life. So, Islam as a system is something that Sire talks about.

Sire calls it Islamic Theism - because it is Theism - but it is very important to recognise that Islamic Theism is not falling or coming from the same 'tree' as Christian Theism. Islamic Theism is a description of God's identity according to Mohammed, not according to God Himself. So, we have a description of Theism by a man who we would believe has been heavily influenced by God's enemies - Satan and his kingdom. We would not subscribe in any way to Islamic Theism and if we define the answers to those eight questions, it would be enough for us to say that Islamic Theism is very, very different to Christian Theism. It is substantially and irreconcilably different to Christian Theism.

Animism

Animism is a belief that we run into around the world. It is a kind of pantheism, but it describes the actions and activity of spirit forces in the world around us that inhabit even inanimate objects, but certainly animate objects - spirits that inhabit animals and other things, and that control life around us. Many, many of the minority (people group) worldview systems, even if they have an overlay of a high religion - Christianity or Islam, etc. - there is a significant component of Animism in their daily life.

We can apply those eight questions to the mind of an Animist and we would come up with a common set of responses that Animists offer to those questions.

Another model of worldview

Now we are going to move on from looking at specific worldviews and look at an adaptation of the 'orange circle model' that we already saw - the one that had worldview in the centre and moved out toward behaviour. We are going to describe that model with a different set of terms. In the book that was written by Wilkens and Sanford, we are pointed toward a different 'take' on the model of worldview.

This model begins with the concept of *Story*. That is important for us because in our way of working cross-culturally, we are very intent on people understanding God's Grand Story. We are very intent on describing God's Story for them so that they can evaluate God's Story and they can determine how they can connect with God's Story. That is an important thing for us.

As we have discussed, worldviews in fact do arise from stories - at the centre of life is a story - for every human being. We each have a story, and the informal influences of our societies, our 'nature and nurture' - who we are and what our culture tells us - those things help to determine what our worldviews actually are. They shape our worldviews and so those are part of our story. Those stories that we each have, create an identity for us. Our identities are concepts for us that include: what it means to be successful, what it means to be fulfilled, how do we really fit in to the system of meaning around us?

So, we would consider the inner circle in this model to be 'story', the secondary circle to be our 'identity': the identity that derives from our story. The third layer is our 'convictions' - those things which are a distillation of our story and that form the framework of propositions that we operate on the basis of - very similar to 'beliefs' in the other model. Then, from our convictions we derive something we talked about before, our 'values' or our 'ethics'. Our beliefs about nature and how reality works radiate out and shape our ethics, which is what we should do, and what we prioritise in our lives to do.

Values and ethics are a more practical application of our underlying statements of conviction. Then as we live out our values and our ethics we come to the last layer which is our 'morals' and 'actions'. This is the part of the story that is the most evident to other people, and the part of the story that actually shows the outworking of our own personal story. So to summarise each area in the model:

Story: The central narrative of our life
Identity: How we see ourselves and present ourselves to others
Convictions: Those beliefs that make up how reality works for us
Values/Ethics: What we believe we should do and what we take to be our highest priorities

Morals/Actions: The realm of doing that includes all of our activities

God's Story

Our worldviews need to be framed within the context of God's Story. That is our desire - to see people's worldviews realigned and framed in the context of God's Grand Narrative. In order for people to be able to do that, they have to see an adequate unfolding of God's Narrative - to be able to evaluate and ask questions about it so that they can see the explanatory power of God's Narrative - His Story. They can see that His Story leads to an identity for Him and they can see that His identity describes a set of values or convictions of God (even though God is the definition of Truth). Then they can see that in His actions, He is consistently working from the basis of His character - it is a defining point of His convictions and His values, and of God Himself, who He is - on the basis of His Narrative, His Story. So we want other human beings in other societies to see how their story fits in the big picture of God's Story. How their stories are threads, interwoven into God's Story and His design.

The informal, narrative nature of worldview is one of the reasons why our teaching approach is so effective. Because we take the time to very progressively present - in story form - an alternative to the worldviews that animists particularly, but many people, have bought into. We present a cohesive, a holistic, Story with much greater explanatory power, that answers the major questions of life. We present that in a narrative fashion that helps people to make a decision about the 'rebuild' of their core identity on the basis of the identity of who God is. So, we want to know what these competing worldviews are saying, and then we want to present God's Grand Narrative in a way that people can evaluate that Narrative and determine how their lives and life experiences are actually more compatible with God's Narrative than they are with the narratives that they have previously accepted.

DISCUSSION POINTS

1. The tutorial mentions how the idea of 'tolerance' as a cultural law has come out of *Postmodernism* - a rejection of the absolutes of science and religion. What are some ways, if any, in which you can see the 'law of tolerance' affecting:

- the society around you
- the church
- your own thinking

 ACTIVITIES

1. Watch the following video of young Australians, who hold to a variety of worldviews, discussing various questions of life - http://youtu.be/zCSYWWEQp-s. As you watch, think about how their values, ethics and convictions are shaped by the overarching story that each has accepted as their own story - their own identity.

Worldviews 4

OBJECTIVES OF THIS TUTORIAL

This tutorial is the fourth and final one focusing on worldview. We will look at some of the more informal worldview influences at work in our society that may affect the way we think. We will also look at four important questions to ask about any worldview to see if it "works".
The notes were transcribed from a video presentation, so watch the video as you read the notes.

Last Time

We looked at some of the major, common worldviews that Sire describes as a result of applying those eight questions to the human view of life in many societies.

The second set of worldview issues we are going to describe now, will be in terms of the less formalised model, (from Wilkens and Sanford) that we looked at last time - the one with Story at the centre. We said that the *story* develops an *identity* for each individual, which in turn derives into a set of *convictions*, and that those convictions create *values* and *ethics* (ways that we define our priorities and what we believe to be the most important things to do). Then, our *morals* and our *actions* are the 'doing' that results in our activities from our story, our identity, our convictions and our values.

These two authors are saying that we don't take in worldviews as formalised systems that are a cohesive or coherent package that we intellectually evaluate, then accept. That almost never happens - that's not the way worldviews are adopted. They are adopted informally, piecemeal, they change, morph, grow, shrink in certain areas, they are based on our own personal stories in society, in cultural contexts. Those cultural influences have a high degree of involvement and interaction with the development of our worldviews.

We are going to build on that idea by looking at another set of worldview categories.

Describing some informal worldview categories

These worldview categories are not comparatively religious - they are not about the comparison between Hinduism and Islam, or the Muslim and Christian worldviews. These worldviews, as Wilkens and Sanford describe them, are about the means in Western society by which we define what ultimately redeems our existence.

Many of these things are informal. They are bought into because they are the societal or political influences that drive our societies. They are not even necessarily developed as rationally coherent systems - in other words that we have made sure that there is no contradiction between the components and therefore we accept them. No, these are very informal, very culturally derived - and, they make a very good point - that the church is not at all immune to this kind of worldview influence. These worldview influences do affect believers and affect Christians in ways that we are surprised by, and if we are not careful to evaluate our lives we find ourselves unknowingly buying into key components of these worldviews.

This is important because we want to have a story that is an outworking of God's Grand Story, of His Narrative. We don't want to be surprised one day that we promoted something - for example something as heinous as slavery, which many Christians did promote - and then to find that it is inconsistent with a true Christian Theism or truly Christian worldview. So, we don't want to be taken by surprise by not understanding what our worldviews actually consist of.

We are going to look at some worldview categories, and we will look at them, not using Sire's eight questions, but from the point of view of Wilkens and Sanford, by looking at the minimal, most important component.

Individualism

I am at the centre. My happiness is at the centre. 'Salvation' is found in me being happy - my fulfilment is salvation. The American Constitution and some of the early American documents from the Deists who wrote those - Thomas Jefferson and others (who, ironically, many Christians quote, even though they were Deists and we couldn't ever buy into that) - uphold that strong sense of individualism, that the pursuit of happiness is our right and it is a divine right. It is something that drives our societies and it turns into pragmatism - 'leveraging relationships' for an ulterior motive, for example in business models. Even in the Christian community we hear talk of that kind of thing and we are alarmed by it - at least some of us are.

So, Individualism defines us at the centre and creates a cold pragmatism that says: 'what is in my best interests is what is best'. That means that I have to operate in the context of my political and social environment and 'get along', yes, but ultimately I am doing that and following the rules in business because if I don't, I will get sent to prison. So, at the end of the day I am going to do what's best for me.

Individualism is a very strong value in American society and in a lot of situations. It affects Christians and creates a relative standard of right and wrong in practical terms for people, because it is about what is best for me at the end of the day - what I can get away with, too (unfortunately). So, Individualism: salvation is found in the fulfilment of the individual - my happiness fulfilled.

Consumerism

I am what I own. It is very subtle, but it is very strong in our societies. Branding, advertising, the association of our identity with the things that we own, the things that are in our house, that we drive, that we wear - consumerism is a big issue. As we said, it is like a means of salvation. Defining our story and our identity on the basis of fulfilment or salvation as provided by my identity showing off what I own and what possessions I am associated with. It's crazily non-Christian, but we buy into this. We see this all the time in the church, in Christian circles, in 'society' - the pomp and circumstance view of competing with the neighbours for the nicer car, or nicer house or nicer boat or the nicer

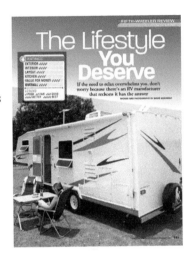

clothes or the prettier family or whatever... So, Consumerism very much affects us.

Nationalism

Nationalism may affect Americans more than Australian or British culture. Nationalism - 'my nation under God', or as Bob Dylan said, 'Those who go to war, feel like they go to war because God is on their side'. Have you ever heard of a conflict in which one country says, 'God is not on our side but we are going to fight anyway', whereas the other country says, 'Well, God is on our side, so we have greater likelihood of winning.' Nobody goes and says, 'It is not our destiny to win'. Ironically, in the same competition, two different people will be praying and depending on God's intervention to help them to be successful, even in war and conflict.

So, in American society ('my nation under God') there is a strong relationship between conservative, political philosophy and conservative religious philosophy. Those things are closely tied together - if I am conservative religiously, I am conservative politically. If I am conservative religiously, then they would be shocked to hear that I am a 'liberal' politically - that is incompatible in American national identity, in most circles. Nationalism becomes part of the fabric of Christian identity in many American situations, because of a close allegiance with the idea that 'my nation has a manifest or divine destiny'. Wilkens and Sanford point out (tongue in cheek) several areas where, if you view the divine destiny of the American government in a certain kind of way, you are probably a Nationalist. If you think that God's plan will be de-railed if America's role is diminished in the next 25 years, you might be a Nationalist. So, they are helping us to identify those areas of Nationalism.

I was watching the Diamond Jubilee ceremony with the Queen the other day, and although there is no problem with some level of patriotism, defining the world with our nation at the centre is a tell-tale sign of Nationalism, and is certainly not a healthy place for Christians to live. Nationalism often carries with it a salvific message - our identities are defined by our nationhood, our salvation is defined by our nationhood - if our nation is not in the driver's seat, my life has less value. That is something that politicians and others in our societies talk about and believe and promote (which is a bit scary).

Moral Relativism

Relativism says that there is no absolute truth. Relativism gets itself into trouble by claiming *absolutely* that there is no absolute truth - by saying that there is no right or wrong, except that it is absolutely right for me to tell you that there is no right and wrong. That is the one absolute right, the fact that I can tell you to agree with me that there is no right and wrong. That is the kind of circular thinking that happens in Relativism.

Relativism is very prevalent in our societies. The guilt that is placed upon us, (especially as believers, if we defend Truth, or defend absolutes) is very strong. In TV and in the media, things that we read, and in conversations that we have out in society - if you do not hold to some humble sense of relativism, then you are an arrogant person who has no business out and about talking and dealing with people. You need to accept relativism and not try to force your ideas on someone else - that is the characterisation that gets made.

Scientific Naturalism

Scientific Naturalism says that 'only matter matters'. Wilkens and Sanford state that they don't want to include comparative religion in their study, because it would just be too long a book. Scientific Naturalism, however, is saying that if there is any salvation for humankind, it is through science. They describe what Scientific Naturalism means to our societies - the strong and militant push you see in certain circles for evolution as the only acceptable view - that any Creationist view is just utter nonsense. That view is being promoted so strongly and so militantly - everything you watch on TV for example, assumes evolution. Scientific Naturalism is a very strong influence on our societies today.

New Age

Are we actually gods ourselves, or are we God's creation? The New Age is seeking identity and salvation through 'spirituality' in all those ways we have already described - in a psychic, mystical, extra-sensory perception, occultic world. It is a different kind of salvation through the reduction to the means of New Age religion.

Postmodern Tribalism

Postmodernism tends to create an environment where relativity is king, where tolerance is the rule, and yet Postmodern Tribalists have to find salvation and an identity somewhere. What we see happening with Postmodernists is that they become "tribal". Postmodern Tribalism sounds like a self-contradiction. We see, for example, that Feminist rhetoric and Feminist literature is everywhere in Postmodernism - in Postmodern studies, Feminism comes to the forefront constantly. Why is that? Because Feminists have an agenda - they believe that their 'oppression' has been historically connected to other philosophical views and that people have not been tolerant of them in the past. They believe that their agenda needs to be promoted so that people will be more tolerant of them and so they talk and write in sometimes very militant terms about that view: that tolerance is the rule, but you do not have the right to be intolerant of me - you are required to be tolerant of me. I don't have to be tolerant of the fact that you are not tolerant of me. It sounds circular, and it tends to be circular.

Tolerance is the rule for life. That is the view of the Postmodern Tribalist, and we see that return to tribalism in our Postmodern society. People cannot exist in a 'tolerance vacuum' - it is not possible - they have to define themselves, they have to define their core identities in conjunction with society - that is the way God has made them. So as much as people try to create a neutral, value-free environment for themselves to live in, at the end of the day,  their natural bent and penchant for definition requires them to move toward defining identities. That is the way God has made them. Unfortunately, if they reject God at the starting point, their salvation gets defined in other terms. Postmodern Tribalists find their salvation in their core identities, over and against the lack of tolerance that others are showing to them. Their identity gets defined by that intolerance of others itself - which is quite a bizarre twist to things - because that defies the Postmodern view itself.

Salvation by Therapy

Wilkens and Sanford use the quote: "Not as good as it gets" - this is a quote from a movie where a guy is dealing with psychologists and therapists, and he is trying to find the cure for his problems through therapy, with psychologists and psychiatrists. Wilkens and Sanford are saying that in society, many times salvation gets reduced to the psychological component and that people try to find their salvation or their restoration through the health of their psyche - their psychological make-up.

Wilkens and Sanford are contending that, in contrast to all of these informal world-views, Christianity *includes* all those elements, but it doesn't reduce life to one specific area. It doesn't reduce life to 'my happiness'. It doesn't reduce life to 'my physical needs being met' (as in Consumerism). It doesn't reduce life to 'my security and safety in national identity' (as in Nationalism). It doesn't reduce life to the relative relationship of 'I need you to be tolerant of me and treat me with respect' (as in Moral Relativism). It doesn't reduce life to scientific explanations (as in Scientific Naturalism). It doesn't reduce life to spirituality only (as in the New Age movement). It doesn't reduce life to tribalism (as in Postmodern Tribalism) or to salvation by therapy. They are saying that all of those components, in balance, are encapsulated in the Christian Theistic world-view, but these worldviews distort reality by over-emphasising specific components of life. So, they have given a list of these informal cultural influences on our lives that we need to be aware of, and which help us to evaluate our own worldviews. Because, as we said in the beginning, the starting point for us in the evaluation of our own worldviews.

Evaluating our own worldview

If we want to evaluate a worldview, we use Sire's questions, we hear someone's story told, or we evaluate our own story and we apply Sire's questions to our story and we see the outworking of our worldview. Most of you would have clear answers to Sire's questions - all except the last one - which is: 'What core commitments manifest them-selves as a result of your answers to those first seven questions?' Those of us who are Christian Theists would answer the first seven questions the same way, but, the core commitments that result in practical outworking - our morals and our actions - do not necessarily look the same. We may find, that in that specific area, we need to evaluate our worldviews more in accordance with Wilkens and Sanford's list, to see if...'Wait a second, in practice, my life is pretty Individualist - or it is pretty Consumerist...I actually have some Nationalistic thinking that is built into my core commitments'.

Which challenges us to go back to this worldview model that is centred on our story and our core identity and to evaluate our identity correctly. Because, our Christian allegiance should create an identity centred in the person of Jesus Christ and what He has for us, but it doesn't always happen that way.

Wilkens and Sanford are challenging us in a more informal way, to answer that eighth question, about our core commitments in terms of what our morals and our actions actually demonstrate - and that is a good challenge for us.

That is the way we describe worldview, it is a way we can understand a bit more about our own core commitments and our own identity. But, as we apply ourselves to other worldviews - as we look at animists in minority society, as we look at the Islamic worldview, as we look at Naturalism - what kind of questions can we use to critique or evaluate those systems of thought? That's where we are headed now.

Worldview Coherence

Here are four questions that we can use to evaluate worldviews around us:

1. Is it rationally coherent?

Is the worldview rationally coherent? Is it non-contradictory, or do individuals with this worldview hold to two components that tend to be contradictory?

Closed systems - those that don't allow for a transcendent input or a transcendent standard - tend, by definition, to be contradictory. For example, for a Naturalist - a person who believes that all there is, is in the 'box', that there is no voice speaking into the box with any standard - has a very difficult time explaining right and wrong, or human rationality, or meaning, in a way that isn't contradictory with this deterministic, cause-and-effect system that they are adhering to. They can't say how a naturalistic causation of evolution produces beings who value certain things and don't value other things, who have a sense of right and wrong and a sense of self - they can't describe how that actually happens in terms of their own system. They can tell you what 'should be' or what 'can be', for example, they can tell you that a lion can kill a zebra, but they can't tell you what 'ought to be'. They can't tell you why a human being 'ought not' to kill an-other human being. They don't have an explanation for moving from what can be done to what ought to be done. That requires a transcendent standard - someone speaking into the box. That creates rational incoherence, which manifests itself in contradiction between the presuppositions of the worldview and what we are seeing in practise in the lives around us.

Animists do not tend to evaluate their worldviews in terms of rational coherence. There are a lot of rational contradictions in the animistic worldviews that I have been exposed to. For example, believing that a plant that cannot hear, and doesn't show any signs, in any way that we can imagine, of being able to react to us not following the proper ceremonies for it to grow, they still believe, in spite of that evidence, that if I don't do the right incantations, that plant won't grow well.

A rationally coherent worldview is one that is non-contradictory, and closed systems tend to produce rational incoherence.

2. Is it empirically correspondent to reality, covering the whole of life in an adequate way?

Reductionist or Absolutising worldviews - like the ones Wilkens and Sanford talk about, which reduce salvation or the means of fulfilment to a small component of the whole of human life: to psychology, or matter, or spirituality, or to our national identity, or to our tribalistic identity as in Postmodernism, or to Moral Relativism, or to Individualism or Consumerism - that reduce life to one area, do not provide a system that is empirically holistic - that covers the whole of life.

All worldviews, whether people admit it or not, are plans of salvation or redemption. They are ways to redeem back the problems of pain and suffering in life. That is why science makes the claims that it makes, they say they can solve life's problems. So, these are systems of salvation or redemption, and we are saying that those are not empirically correspondent to reality - they fail to explain the whole of our reality in an adequate way. For example, they fail to explain the existence of evil - they can't explain that. We can explain the existence of evil because a good God created perfect beings and He gave them a choice, and their choices led them to rebel against Him - He was not the person who created evil, but evil resulted as a consequence of the choices that were made by others. That is an explanation of the existence of evil, but many systems can't explain the existence of evil. They can't explain absolute rights and wrongs, they can't explain truth, they can't explain knowledge, etc. So they don't empirically correspond to reality.

3. Is it existentially consistent, liveable and functional?

Can you live that way? Is it liveable and functional? We already said that Naturalism or Relativism is very difficult to live. For a Nihilist, an adequate response is suicide, because there is no meaning to reality, there is no reason why I should respect and love my wife, as opposed to abusing my wife. There is no reason why I should drive on the side of the road that has been defined by the government as opposed to just doing whatever I want. There is no reason why I should avoid a car wreck as opposed to being in a car wreck. There is no reason why I should wear clothes as opposed to not wearing clothes. Ultimately there is no reason. So, that is a system that is very difficult to live out because we are forced to live in systems of meaning while at the same time, claiming there is no meaning.

It is the same with Relativism - we are forced to live in systems of truth and right and wrong,

while at the same time claiming that there is no such thing. As one philosopher said, even in India, where people claim that truth is relative in some of the systems that are there, if you cross the street and there is a bus coming, either you get out of the way of the bus or if you stand in the way of the bus, it kills you. The law of contradiction is not negotiable. You can't define a worldview system that is not practically liveable - that is not an adequate worldview. It needs to be existentially consistent.

4. Is it emotively compelling, addressing our heart-level questions?

Is the worldview emotively compelling? Does it address the heart-level questions that we have?

We have already stated, as Sire has explained, those kinds of questions about meaning, about truth, about right and wrong, about our existences, about the 'whys' of life - those are questions that human beings ask time and time again, around the world, culture to culture, age to age - they do not change.

Some worldviews just do not answer our heart-level questions. They provide us with a sense of futility, a sense of meaninglessness, a sense of nonsense and chaos. A worldview needs to be emotively compelling. It needs to address our heart-level questions.

? DISCUSSION POINTS

1. When you evaluate your own worldview, do you see any of the influences mentioned in the tutorial affecting you in any way, or have they affected you at some point in your life? (Individualism, Consumerism, Nationalism, Moral Relativism, etc.)

2. Do you think it is possible for a Christian to live in our society without being in some way affected by the prevailing worldview around them?

➡ ACTIVITIES

1. The following links are for two different presentations of aspects of the Christian Theist worldview. The second one discusses the effect of Postmodernism on the Church. It was uploaded in 2007 - can you note any movement in the effect of postmodern thinking in the church since that time?

http://youtu.be/Txez9sJUtaE

http://youtu.be/gv6uxCch7oc

Evaluating Worldviews

This tutorial begins to explore the intersection between 'cultural values' and 'worldview', and looks at some of the challenges in evaluating or making judgments about a person's worldview simply from their behaviour.

Introduction

We are going to first take a look at some of the cultural values you hold personally, and have you link those to specific actions or activities that you engage in. Then we will look at some of the challenges in understanding or evaluating another person's worldview.

Your own 'culture'

In this activity, you are asked to identify your own, personal, position on the following eight continuums that describe fundamental areas of culture. The descriptions below refer to overall cultural values, but you should think about how much each pole of the value matches your own. Mark your position on the continuum to identify your personal value.

After noting your position, write an example that describes how the value being expressed has actually *outworked* itself in specific ways in your life - how it has been displayed in attitudes or actions. For example, if you hold more to a polychronic than a monochronic value of time, you probably tend not to worry so much about being 'late'. For each area, think about whether your value is a direct result of your Christian Theistic worldview, or is a 'cultural value'.

Self Identification

Primary identification is with one's self. The self is the smallest unit of survival. Self-reliance, personal freedom and emotional distance from others are important. Protecting one's self guarantees the well being of others. Identity is a function of one's own achievements.

Group Identification

Identity is the function of group membership. The smallest unit of survival is the primary group. Interdependence and looking after the group, insures the well being of the individual.

People need close affiliation with others. Too much freedom is scary.

Egalitarian Mentality

An egalitarian mentality is the norm. Group membership is casual and voluntary. No strong sense of in/outgroup exists. Most people are treated the same. People are informal with friends and strangers alike. It's easy to change groups and make friends.

Ingroup Mentality

An ingroup mentality prevails. People are close and intimate with their ingroup, and compete with their outgroup. They're formal with all but their ingroup. People have little trust of the outgroup. Groups hardly change. It's harder to make friends.

Autonomous

Autonomous organisations prevail. Workers are more independent. Individuals receive recognition, and decision-making is by majority rule. Loyalty from/to the organisation is less; results are key and people are rewarded according to their contribution to the organisation.

Collective

Collective organisations prevail. Teamwork, cooperation, group recognition and loyalty to/from the organisation are the norm. Decision-making is by consensus. Harmony is key. Rewards are distributed equally.

Universalism

Universalism is the rule. Personal and societal obligations are of equal importance and should be balanced. Rules should be applied equally to the ingroup and society in general. What is right is always right, regardless of circumstances. Objectivity is valued and expected.

Particularism

Particularism prevails. It's necessary to distinguish between ingroup and societal obligations; the former are important, the latter less so. Being fair is to treat the ingroup well and let others fend for themselves. What is right depends on the situation. Context is crucial. Subjectivity is valued and expected.

Monochronic (time focus)   **Polychronic (people focus)**

←————————————————————————————————→

People's attitude towards time is monochronic. People must adjust to the demands of time; time is limited. Sometimes people are too busy to see you. People live by the external clock.

A polychronic attitude towards time is the norm. Time is bent to meet the needs of people. They're never too busy; there's always more time. People live by an internal clock.

One thing at a time   **Many things at once**

←————————————————————————————————→

People do things one at a time. They stand in line; they expect undivided attention. Interruptions are bad; schedules, deadlines are important. Late is bad; adherence to schedule is the goal. Plans are not easily changed.

People do many things at one time. People stand in line less. Divided attention is okay. Interruptions are life. Schedules and deadlines are considered a loose guide. Late is late. Completing the transaction is the goal. Plans can be easily changed.

Life is what I do   **Life is what happens to me**

←————————————————————————————————→

There are few givens in life, few things I can't change and must accept. I can be/do whatever I want, if I make the effort. My happiness is up to me. Unhappiness is not normal. Human beings are the locus of control.

There are some things I have to live with; there may be limits to what I can do/be; happiness and unhappiness are normal parts of life. Human beings are only sometimes the locus of control.

Progress is inevitable   **Progress is not automatic**

←————————————————————————————————→

Change is usually for the better. Tradition is not always right. Optimism is best. Technology is often the answer. Every problem has a solution. New is usually better.

Change can be for the worse. Realism is best. Tradition is a good guide. Some problems can't be solved. Technology does not have all the answers. New is not necessarily better.

Now read again each of the things you wrote as examples of how your values have played out in your real life actions or attitudes. Do you think that someone who didn't know you would be able to understand your Story (worldview) from these things alone?

What would it take for someone to understand your core identity and worldview - and how easily do you think someone could misunderstand your true identity by only judging you by your actions?

Two Stories

Look at the photo to the right of a group of people protesting a supermarket development in a small Australian town. Imagine that you are visiting this town and come upon this scene. What are your initial impressions - just from observing - about these people and the values they might possibly hold, what *kind* of people do you think they are? What conclusions can you to come to about their convictions, identity or worldview? Remember our orange circle model with Story at the centre? Let's use it to trace back some different *possible* scenarios for the Story of two of the people in the photograph.

Caroline's Story

Morals/Actions: I attended a protest against a new supermarket development in my area.

Values/Ethics: If I don't do something, then who will? This new development will increase traffic and pollution, and lower my quality of life. We each create our own meaning, pleasure, and prosperity in life and so I have to stand up for my rights.

Convictions: Man should live by whatever values he deems best for his own happiness and the survival of the human race.

Identity: There is no god and no moral absolutes, so human life has no transcendent meaning.

Story: Naturalistic philosophy and scientific method supply all real knowledge.

John's Story

Morals/Actions: I attended a protest against a new supermarket development in my area.

Values/Ethics: I think it is important to communicate my views publicly in the right way - this new development will destroy an important wetland in our area which is the home of the birds that live there - and they are a valuable part of God's creation. Christians should show that they care about relevant community issues.

Convictions: Man has a responsibility to look after the things on earth that God gave us and that He values. We can communicate to others who God is, by the views we publicly express and by finding common ground with them by taking part in community life.

Identity: There is a God who wants people to know Him and the way He provided through His Son, I have a responsibility to try to reach people in my community with that message.

Story: God, an infinite and personal Spirit, created the world and is intimately related to it and to human beings and He gave His Son as a sacrifice for our sin.

Discovering worldviews

So, how do we discover what someone's identity, or worldview, truly is? There is actually a lot we can discover from observation, but ultimately we must actually spend time with the person and get to know the things that they value - by listening to their thoughts and relating to them as they live life - to really understand *who they are* inside.

If we had an opportunity to talk to John and Caroline, we would probably begin to understand that they had different motivations for being there. We would know even more, if we could meet their families and take part in some life activities with them and understand their point of view on a variety of other subjects. Our tendency might be to initially categorize all of the protesters as 'left-wing greenies' or 'environmental activists' - whether we think positively or negatively about it, we still tend to assume we know a fair bit about their motivations. Why do we do that? Because we have an existing frame of reference for 'people who take part in protests' - so our initial thoughts about the protesters' values is based on our knowledge of the cultural framework that we have for this kind of protest, and what it probably means in the context of Australian culture and life. Human beings do not very often go into a situation thinking - 'I probably don't fully understand what is going on here and need to find out more to really understand', but that is how we should always approach others, especially those of another culture.

Having an understanding of a broader cultural framework and context, including commonly held cultural values, *does* help us. It provides a *starting point* - a point of intersection for us to be able to communicate with people in a culturally appropriate way, in language they understand, and about things that we can both relate to. *Then* we can begin to develop a relationship based on a real understanding of where someone is 'coming from'.

❓ DISCUSSION POINTS

1. Do you think that the Christian Theistic worldview that we hold to, guides us in all areas of culture and values, such as those mentioned in the tutorial continuums? To what extent?

2. Jesus said the first and greatest commandment was to "love the Lord your God with all your heart and with all your soul and with all your mind", and that the second is "You shall love your neighbour as yourself" - Matt 22:37-39. Which area of the 'orange circle' do you think is Jesus talking about here, and why?

➡️ ACTIVITIES

1. Submit the notes and examples from the continuum exercise in the tutorial.

6.6 Culture threads

This tutorial introduces a framework for describing cultures - culture threads.

Introduction

As we saw in the last tutorial, each society and culture is made up of many different 'personal cultures' of individuals, which differ because of religious, regional, gender, work or other factors.

So how can we look at the various factors that *are* common to that culture or that are representative of that particular culture? In this tutorial we are going to identify some general categories that we can use to look at the commonly held cultural values and some of the *cultural threads* that permeate the lives of each individual within a culture. We will then describe several different cultures using these categories.

Culture 'study'

Over the years, there have been a number of anthropological models developed - with hundreds of separate cultural categories - designed to provide a framework for describing any particular culture in great detail. However, information about people as they live their lives in "real time" in their particular cultural framework does not lend itself naturally to being dissected and recorded in neatly labeled categories. There is something missing - a personal, spontaneous element that doesn't come through in the rather static definition and categorization of objects, actions, systems, rituals, etc. that anthropologists have used.

Anthropological 'culture study' has traditionally seen cultures in a structurally functional - almost scientific - way, concentrating on social organisation and often assuming that there are no moral and cultural absolutes. Each culture is seen as an autonomous and static model that can be recorded as a captured image and then studied in an objective manner, requiring the researcher to remain (mentally at least) *outside* of the culture in order to somehow retain an unbiased view. Unfortunately, this often leads to an unbalanced focus on form (the behaviour of people) to the detriment of consideration of underlying meaning (identity, worldview).

As we have seen, culture and language cannot be separated because language is the verbal expression of culture. In the same way, culture cannot be separated from the lives of people - there is no separate entity or body of information that is 'culture'. We could say that it is impossible to 'study' a culture without knowing and understanding real, living people, and in moving toward becoming a part of their lives. Because just as languages are always in a process of change, cultures too are in a dynamic process of change.

So, in order to 'deal' with the dynamism and interrelatedness of everything in a culture, we need to identify the important threads that help us to find a framework for entering into the thinking of the people who live within that culture. We want to think just as much about how people express themselves, and not only focus on how they organise themselves.

Culture Threads

The following four areas - *Communication*, *Life Values*, *Relationships* and *Identity* - could be an initial description of common threads running through any culture. They can at least provide a framework for beginning to look in more detail at areas that might be important to people and how the culture is expressed through the lives of people. The descriptions under each heading provide some ideas of some things to think about, but are not an exhaustive list as to what might be important in that area in every culture.

1. Communication

Avenues and methods of communication:

Languages: What are the major languages and varieties of languages used? What is the status and comparative use of these languages?

Outside communication: What is the level or status of communication from outside of the society? (e.g. visitors, media)

Literacy levels: What are the available reading materials, languages of literacy, availability of schools? Is literacy related to status, is it a priority?

Verbal and non-verbal communication: Is communication mainly verbal, or are words and gestures used at different times and in different situations? Do eyes, eyebrows, face, tilt of head, hands, posture, space, time, pitch and tone of voice have a large role in conveying meaning?

Spiritual communication: What are the avenues and methods of communication between people and the non-physical world? (e.g. prayer, interaction with spiritual beings)

Levels of communication:

Formal and informal communication: Is there formal and informal discourse? Are there formalised courtesies? Is there commonly conversation between strangers? When is formal and informal discourse used? (e.g. public and private, dependent on relationship)

Role of age, gender and social status: Do all people interact with all others with the same freedom? Is everyone expected to talk, or is there a spokesperson (within families or larger groups)?

Effective and ineffective communication:

Facets of effective communication: When do people listen? Who do they listen to? When do they understand or misunderstand and how is that communicated? What are the identifying factors in effective and ineffective communication - such as the role of respect, empathy, honesty, status and relationship?

2. Life Values

Harmony

Systems to provide harmony: What systems are in place to provide harmony within the society? Social, economic, political? How is disharmony viewed? What is expected, what is enforced? Is bending the rules okay? What do they expect of one another - what is polite behaviour and impolite behaviour - what embarrasses people?

Conformity: What value is put on obedience, conformity and agreement?

Authority

Who has authority: Which people in the society have authority and how is it expressed? (e.g. within families, groups, or whole communities) How is authority gained? (e.g., through age, position, role?)

Power distance: In which areas do people abdicate responsibility to others for decisions? How important are, equality, class, rank, dominance and non-dominance?

Rebellion: How is protest, or rebellion against authority viewed?

Responsibility

Personal or group responsibility: Is personal responsibility or group responsibility more important? What are the tasks or obligations an individual is expected to do independently? What responsibilities do they have as a group? To one another, to outside groups, to the spiritual world?

What is responsible: When would someone be considered an 'irresponsible person'?

Time

Concept of time: Are they monochronic or polychromic? Is time considered a commodity, how do they think about use and misuse of time and management of time? What are the prevailing attitudes to 'wasting' time, waiting, going fast or slow?

Types of time: What is the unity or separation of "work" and "recreation"?

Measurement of time: Do they favour natural (seasons, moons, harvests) or artificial measurement of time?

Routines and habits: What are the established routines for daily, family, and group life? To what degree are routines expected to be followed, and by whom. What are the rhythms of life?

Time frames: What are considered normal time frames within the lifespan, the working day or week, seasons? What are their ideas about past, present and future orientations?

Privacy

Aloneness: What is the concept of 'aloneness'? Is there a desire to be alone, or is there security within a group?

Levels of privacy: Are there variations of behaviour depending on privacy level?

Use of space: What are the concepts of the quantity and quality of space, exclusive and inclusive space, maximum and minimum space?

Security

Fears: What do they express as fears, and how do they attempt to overcome these? What makes them feel insecure? Sickness, uncertainty, loss, weakness, poverty?

Financial, social, physical security: What are acceptable levels of security, and what are the methods of gaining security or safety? What are their sources of security? Knowledge, status, relationships, government, society, organisations?

Priorities

Goals: Which goals are shared and openly talked about?

Success: How is achievement defined? Who is seen as being successful and why?

Values: How much do people comparatively value: a comfortable life, an exciting life, a sense of accomplishment, a world at peace, a world of beauty, equality, family security, freedom, happiness, inner harmony, mature love, national security, pleasure, salvation, self-respect, social recognition, true friendship, wisdom? What other values are important?

Motivations: What are the motivating factors behind behaviour? (e.g. gaining prestige, physical comfort, financial gain, learning and improving individually or as a society, independence or interdependence, establishing friendships, being a role model, adventure or enjoyment, power and influence)

Enculturation

Respect: Who are the most respected people in the community, the ones people listen to?

Important topics: What are common topics of conversation?

Enculturation: How are the values of effective communication passed on? How are ethical/religious values instilled or strengthened? What methods are used to pass on appropriate and acceptable relationship-building skills? How is identity described and consciously or unconsciously communicated? What is the priority of passing on certain values in the society? (e.g. ambition, open-mindedness, competence, neatness, courage, honesty, logic, love, obedience, politeness, dependability, self-control, joyfulness, forgiveness, independence, intelligence, helpfulness)

Changing values: How are values changing and what are the influences for change?

Origin of values - Foundations for ethics

Origins of life: How do their understandings regarding the origins of life affect their values? How does their view of nature affect what they hold in high regard and how they behave toward those things?

History: Do they see history as an unending series of cycles, or as linear? What effect does this have on values? How have specific events in their history affected what they hold in high esteem or low esteem?

Human beings: What is their understanding of the nature of human beings? How does this affect their values?

3. Relationships

Personal interaction

Different levels of interaction: Do all people interact with equal freedom?

Touching: Who touches whom and how? On what occasions?

Getting together: Who visits whom and where? When, where and how do people interact, socialise, converse, eat together, meet, organise events, chat, gather? When do people spend time together? Doing what? Is anyone excluded?

Group interaction: What are the patterns of behaviour with neighbours, guests, bill collectors, business people, schoolteachers, children, policemen, politicians, officials, and family members?

Levels and types of relationships

Groups: What are the distinct groups evident within the society? How do they relate to one another? What are the relationships between individuals of the same or different age, gender, social status, family groups?

Signs of relationship: How do different relationships manifest themselves at different times and in different situations? (i.e., what are the obligations of a relationship - gift exchange, authority, respect, formal language?)

Scope of relationships: How many relationships does a person typically develop and with whom? (e.g. family, other ties, business, formal)

Relationships with those outside the society

Patterns of behaviour to outsiders: What are the different types of outside relationships? What is the purpose and value of outside relationships?

Attitudes to outsiders: Who do they fear, socialize with, scorn, suspect, accept?

Forming and breaking of relationships

Forming relationships: What is the progression of a relationship developing, what are the possible bases for relationships forming, do people think about obligation, mutual dependence, etc.? What are the formal and informal aspects of relationship development?

Relationship breakdown: What are the reasons for and attitudes toward relationship breakdown?

Patterns: What are the real and ideal patterns for relationships in the society?

Relationships between the physical and the spiritual world

Religions: What are the formal and informal aspects of religion in the society, and the varieties of religious belief? What are some examples of individual or group relations with spiritual beings? What are some of the attitudes and understanding - beliefs - about the spiritual world?

Specialists: Are there religious specialists, priests, pastors, etc.?. What are the attitudes to these people from others within the society - fear, respect or lack of respect?

4. Identity

Individualism and community

Individualism: Does an individual make decisions on his own? Are group beliefs and decisions accepted by all? How much freedom does the individual have, and in which areas? Is individual action socially encouraged?

Perception of oneself: How does a person identify themselves in relation to others? What is their self concept, self respect? How much importance is attached to personal freedom? Does an individual have emotional security?

Competition and affiliation: Is there cooperation and when would people cooperate, or be non-cooperative and individualistic? When would there be group-oriented actions? What would they see as group-identifying factors? Are some criteria more important than others? What is the group proud of? What do they consider a 'scandal', a 'tragedy'? What do they complain about? What are they ashamed of?

Boundaries

Ingroup and outgroup: What are the boundaries of their perception of who is 'one of them' and who isn't? When is someone seen as an outsider? When is someone accepted into the society?

Position in the world: What is their understanding or perception of their place in the wider world? What do they see as their position in wider society? How do they identify themselves to an 'outsider'? Are they defensive? Critical? Complementary?

Foreigners: How do they view those of other races and cultures?

Roles

Roles: What are the major recognised roles in society? Is everyone expected to have a community role? What part does each person play in the society?

Origin of roles: Are they acquired at birth? Tied to social status, gender? Are they assigned, and by whom? Defined by personality, imposed by government, schools, church?

Changing Roles: Are roles shifting or evolving within the society? Have the expectations for certain roles changed? What are some of the attitudes or consequences to role changes?

➡ ACTIVITIES

1. Choose one of the subheading sections of the Culture Threads outline (e.g., *Avenues and methods of communication, Authority, Individualism and community,* etc.). Do a brief write-up on your own culture using the questions under the subheading you chose.

2. Now, using the same subheading you used above, try to find Bible verses that describe Biblical culture for the points mentioned.

3. After you have completed the activities above, think about how people from different cultures might interpret the Bible through their own cultural framework.

6.7 Culture snapshots 1

OBJECTIVES OF THIS TUTORIAL

This tutorial looks at two different cultures - Jamaican and South Korean - by giving a brief description of some of the things that are important to people in those cultures, and some of the culture threads that are evident in their societies.

Introduction

We are going to take a snapshot - a brief look at - two different cultures. Our purpose isn't to stereotype or pigeonhole the individuals within those societies. We simply want to look at some common threads in each one in order to develop an overall picture of the fact that different cultures handle the same issues and problems in a variety of ways. We also want you to think about your own perceptions as an outsider and how those views have been formed.

Jamaica

 Before you read our brief introduction to some aspects of Jamaican culture, think about what you already know and think about Jamaican people - and the stereotypes you may already have in mind. How were your views formed?

1. Communication

Language: English (official), and Creole. English is the official language of Jamaica. However, Patois (Creole), a combination of English and some African languages, is spoken in rural areas and is used increasingly in urban areas. Most Jamaicans can speak or understand Patois, but there are few written materials in Patois. The Bible was translated into Patois in 2011 - you can read a story about it here: http://www.bbc.co.uk/news/magazine-16285462. Jamaican speech, even in English, has a distinctive rhythmic and melodic quality.

The most common greeting is the handshake with direct eye contact, and a warm smile. You can hear a local introducing some common greetings in Jamaican Patois here: http://youtu.be/9Xw58FC8T78

Once a friendship has been established, women may hug and kiss on each cheek, starting with the right. Men often pat each other's shoulder or arm during the greeting process or while conversing.

People are addressed by their honorific title (Mr, Mrs, or Miss) and their surname until a personal relationship has developed. It is normal to wait until invited before using someone's first name. As friendship deepens, a person may be asked to call someone else by their nickname.

Jamaicans can be direct communicators and are not afraid to say what they think. They expect others to be equally direct. At the same time, they value tact and sensitivity and dislike overt aggression. They will politely tell you what they think, even if they dis-agree with what you have said. They appreciate brevity and are not impressed by too much detail. When dealing with people at the same level, communication can be more informal.

Jamaicans stand very close when conversing. A man may touch the arm or shoulder of another man, or even touch his lapel, while speaking.

2. Life Values

Jamaicans have a healthy distrust of those in authority and prefer to put their faith in those they know well, such as their extended family and close friends who are treated as if they were family. This can be seen in the fact that many still prefer to form a "partner" with friends and family rather than go to a bank to secure a loan. A partner is a finan-cial arrangement between friends and neighbours. Each person in the group agrees to contribute a set amount into the partner for a specific number of weeks. Accumulated funds are used to make down payments for large purchases such as buying a house or a business. The basic requirement of the partner is trust. To become a member of the elite group, a person must be recommended by a friend or relative.

Jamaicans value logic and linear thinking. They expect punctuality although they are not always successful at arriving on time themselves.

3. Relationships

Relationships are viewed as more important than rules. The Jamaican family includes a close-knit web of aunts, uncles, cousins and grandparents. Families are close and provide both emotional and economic support to its members.

Although it is not imperative that you be introduced by a third-party, such introduc-tions can speed up the time it takes to develop the personal relationship so necessary to conducting business successfully.

Networking and relationship building are crucial. While Jamaicans are outwardly warm and friendly, they often appear standoffish at the initial introduction because they are reserved until they get to know someone. Socialising is an important part of developing a relationship.

Status is respected in Jamaica. It is quite common to hear someone referred to as "bossman" or "bosswoman" when the person addressing them is not an employee. It is imperative to show deference and respect to those in positions of authority.

4. Identity

Ethnic Make-up: black 90.9%, East Indian 1.3%, white 0.2%, Chinese 0.2%, mixed 7.3%, other 0.1%.

Religions: Protestant 61.3% (Church of God 21.2%, Baptist 8.8%, Anglican 5.5%, Seventh-Day Adventist 9%, Pentecostal 7.6%, Methodist 2.7%, United Church 2.7%, Brethren 1.1%, Jehovah's Witness 1.6%, Moravian 1.1%), Roman Catholic 4%, other including some spiritual cults 34.7%.

The family is the most important group a person belongs to, and as such, it is the group with whom a person spends most of his/her time developing and maintaining cordial relations.

Religion is fundamental to Jamaican life, which can be seen in the references to Biblical events in everyday speech. The island has the highest number of churches per capita in the world and more than 100 different Christian denominations. Most Jamaicans say they are Christians; the largest denominations are the Anglicans, Baptists, Methodists, Pentecostals, Brethren and Roman Catholics.

Christmas is typically observed by various denominations with Communion services, candlelight ceremonies, concerts, all-night prayer meetings and the singing of Christmas carols.

There are three types of Rastafarians in Jamaica; Rastafarians believe they are one of the lost tribes of Israel who were sold into slavery and taken to Babylon (Jamaica) and that they must return to Zion, which they hold to be Ethiopia. The movement does not have organized congregations, it does not have a paid clergy, and it doesn't have a written doctrine.

Find out more about Jamaican culture here:
http://jamaica-guide.info/past.and.present/culture/
Or go here for maps, charts and other information:
http://www.joshuaproject.net/countries.php?rog3=JM

South Korea

 What views do you already hold about South Korean culture? Do you know any South Korean people or perhaps know something of their culture from TV, local restaurants, reading, etc.?

As you read the introduction of Korean culture below, think about how much the four areas - communication, life values, relationships and identity - are interconnected and interwoven and really can't be separated as 'neatly' as we would like.

1. Communication

The Koreans are one ethnic family speaking one language. The Korean language is spoken by more than 65 million people living on the peninsula and its outlying islands as well as 5.5 million Koreans living in other parts of the world. The fact that all Koreans speak and write the same language has been a crucial factor in their strong national identity. Modern Korean has several different dialects including the standard one used in Seoul and central areas, but they are similar enough that speakers and listeners do not have trouble understanding each other.

South Koreans are extremely direct communicators. They are not averse to asking questions if they do not understand what has been said or need additional clarification. This is a culture where "less is more" when communicating. Response to questions is direct and concise. Since there is a tendency to say, "yes" to questions so that there is no loss of face, questions should be phrased so they require a direct response (e.g. It is better to ask, "When can we expect to leave?" than "Can we expect to leave in the next hour?").

Greetings follow strict rules of protocol. Many South Koreans shake hands with expatriates after the bow, thereby blending both cultural styles. The person of lower status bows to the person of higher status, yet it is the most senior person who initiates the handshake. The person who initiates the bow says, "man-na-suh pan-gop-sumnida", which means "pleased to meet you."

Information about the other person will be given to the person they are being introduced to in advance of the actual meeting.

A visitor should wait to be introduced at a social gathering, and when leaving a social gathering, should say good-bye and bow to each person individually.

There is often a strict protocol to be followed when dining as well. A visitor must wait to be told where to sit. The eldest are served first. The oldest or most senior person is the one who starts the eating process.

A person should never point with his chopsticks, or pierce food with them. Chopsticks

should be returned to the table after every few bites or when drinking or speaking. Chopsticks should not be crossed when put on the chopstick rest and should never be placed parallel across the rice bowl. Fruit should be speared with a toothpick. The first offer of second helpings is always refused.

2. Life Values

Family welfare is much more important than the needs of the individual. Members of the family are tied to each other because the actions of one family member reflect on the rest of the family. In many cases the family register can trace a family's history, through male ancestors, for over 500 years.

Kibun is a word with no literal English translation; the closest terms are pride, face, mood, feelings, or state of mind. If you hurt someone's kibun you hurt their pride, cause them to lose dignity, and lose face. Korean interpersonal relationships operate on the principle of harmony.

It is important to maintain a peaceful, comfortable atmosphere at all times, even if it means telling a "white lie". Kibun enters into every facet of Korean life. It is important to know how to judge the state of someone else's kibun, how to avoid hurting it, and how to keep your own kibun at the same time. In business, a manager's kibun is damaged if his subordinates do not show proper respect. A subordinate's kibun is damaged if his manager criticises him in public.

Nunchi is the ability to determine another person's kibun by using the eye. Since this is a culture where social harmony is crucial, being able to judge another person's state of mind is critical to maintain the person's kibun. Nunchi is accomplished by watching body language and listening to the tone of voice as well as what is said.

Koreans may arrive up to 30 minutes late to an invitation without giving offence. Shoes must be removed when entering someone's home.

3. Relationships

The family is the most important part of Korean life. In Confucian tradition, the father is the head of the family and it is his responsibility to provide food, clothing and shelter, and to approve the marriages of family members. The eldest son has special duties: first to his parents, then to his brothers from older to younger, then to his sons, then to his wife, and lastly to his daughters.

The teachings of Confucius describe the position of the individual in Korean society. It is a system of behaviours and ethics that stress the obligations of people towards one another based upon their relationship. The basic tenets are based upon five different relationships:

1) ruler and subject, 2) husband and wife, 3) parents and children, 4) brothers and sisters, and 5) friend and friend. Confucianism stresses duty, loyalty, honour, filial piety, respect for age and seniority, and sincerity.

Gifts express a great deal about a relationship and are always reciprocated. It is inconsiderate to give someone an expensive gift if you know that they cannot afford to reciprocate accordingly. Fruit or good quality chocolates or flowers are appropriate if invited to a Korean's home.

Gifts should be wrapped nicely. The number four is considered unlucky, so gifts should not be given in multiples of four. Giving seven of an item is considered lucky. Gifts should be wrapped in red or yellow paper, since these are royal colours - or yellow or pink paper which denote happiness. Gifts should not be wrapped in green, white, or black paper, and a card shouldn't be signed in red ink. Both hands should be used when offering a gift. Gifts are not opened when received.

South Koreans prefer to do business with people with whom they have a personal connection. It is therefore crucial to be introduced by a third-party. Relationships are developed through informal social gatherings that often involve a considerable amount of drinking and eating.

Individuals who have established mutual trust and respect will work hard to make each other successful. Under no circumstances should someone insult or criticise another person in front of others. Sensitive matters may often be raised indirectly through the intermediary that first made the introductions.

4. Identity

Ethnic Make-up: homogeneous (except for about 20,000 Chinese). Koreans share certain distinct physical characteristics which differentiate them from other Asian people including the Chinese and the Japanese, and have a strong cultural identity as one ethnic family.

Religion: Ancestors are based on the male family line. Children are raised to believe they can never repay their debt to their parents, hence the popularity of ancestor worship. They hold ancestral ceremonies for the previous three generations (parents, grandparents, and great grandparents) several times a year, particularly on Chusok and New Year's Day. On Chusok, people cook and set out food to celebrate their ancestors.

Read this article on the growth of Christianity in South Korea: http://news.bbc.co.uk/2/hi/asia-pacific/8322072.stm

Watch this video made by some university students about 'Korean stereotypes': http://youtu.be/90Y4jx38DF4

Go here for maps, charts and other information: http://www.joshuaproject.net/countries.php?rog3=KS

? DISCUSSION POINTS

1. Based on what you know about the two cultures we have looked at in the tutorial, Jamaica and South Korea, is there one that appeals to you more as a place to live (if you were choosing a place to live)? Why - on what are you basing your preference?

➡ ACTIVITIES

1. Did you notice any *similarities* between the cultures of Jamaica and South Korea? One of the most obvious is the importance placed on "family" in both cultures. There were other similarities as well - list as many of those similarities as you can.

2. There are also obvious differences in the way Jamaicans and South Koreans live and relate to one another. Imagine a family from Jamaica is moving to live in South Korea - what are some of the specific things you think they would find challenging or would need to adjust to?

6.8 Culture snapshots 2

OBJECTIVES OF THIS TUTORIAL

This tutorial looks at two more cultures, those of Finland and Morocco - by giving a brief description of some of the things that are important to people in those cultures, and some of the culture threads that are evident in their societies.

Introduction

We are going to take a snapshot of the cultures of Finland and Morocco. Again, our purpose isn't to stereotype individuals within those cultures, but to look at some common threads in each one to see how people find common solutions to problems and have ways of interacting with one another. We also want you to think again about your own perceptions as an outsider and how your views might have been formed.

Finland

1. Communication

Language: Of the two official languages of Finland, Finnish is the first language spoken by 93% of the country's 5 million inhabitants. Finnish, unlike Scandinavian languages, is not Germanic but in a class of its own. Theoretically, it is related to Hungarian but in practice the two are not mutually comprehensible. The other official language, Swedish, is spoken by around 6% of the population, most of whom live in the southwest and are also speakers of Finnish. Sami is a minority language in Scandinavia that is spoken by around 2,000 people living in the north of Finland, which is 0.03% of the Finnish population.

Finns place a great value on speaking plainly and openly. What someone says is accepted at face value and this is a culture where "a man's word is his bond" and will be treated as seriously as a written contract, so verbal commitments are considered agreements. Finns are direct communicators, and will tell you what they think rather than what you want to hear.

Finns talk in moderate tones and do not do anything to call attention to themselves. Serial conversation is the rule - i.e. listen to the speaker, wait for them to finish and then reply. Interrupting is rude. Greetings are formal, with a firm handshake, direct eye contact, and a smile. It is common practice to repeat your first and surname while shaking hands. When greeting a married couple, the wife should be greeted first.

2. Life Values

Finland is an egalitarian society, which is reflected in their language, which employs gender-neutral words. Finns are very modest and downplay their own accomplishments. They view being humble and modest as virtues. Finns believe there is a proper way to act in any circumstance and always expect courteous behaviour.

Honesty and dependability are the two characteristics held in highest regard among Finns. They do, however, give an extreme degree of space to other people which can mean that the initiative for making friends often falls on a foreigner living in Finland. Once the ice is broken Finns are open and warm. Finns are punctual in both business and social situations.

There is a fairly formal dining etiquette - visitors should wait to be told where to sit.

Table manners are continental; the fork in the left hand and the knife in the right while eating, keeping wrists resting on the edge of the table. Bread and shrimp are the only foods eaten by hand. Even fruit is eaten with utensils. Men should keep their jacket on at meals unless the host removes his. Finns do not appreciate waste, so diners are expected to finish everything on their plate. When finished eating, the knife and fork are placed across the plate with the prongs facing down and the handles facing to the right.

The sauna has a special role in the domestic life of Finns. It is an experience shared with

family and friends. Important business meetings may be followed by a sauna in which the conversation is continued on a more informal basis. Saunas are found everywhere: At the end of the year 2002, there were 1,212,000 saunas in private apartments and another 800,000 in summer cottages and public swimming pools. This translates to more than 2,000,000 saunas for a population of 5.2 million.

3. Relationships

Finns are interested in long-term relationships. Relationship building often takes place outside the work environment: in a restaurant or the sauna. A visitor should realise that it is serious to turn down an invitation to use the sauna, as it is an important part of the Finnish culture.

A century ago most people lived in the countryside. Families had many children, and grandparents were present and participated in caring for, and raising their grandchildren. Even fifty years ago Finnish families were large with many children. People from the rural areas moved increasingly into cities, where construction of compact residential areas was started.

Nowadays a typical Finnish family with children consists of a married mother and father with two children. However, in addition to the nuclear family, there are many different kinds of family. Cohabitation is very common in Finland. There are also many single parent families where children live only with a mother or a father. The number of blended families has also increased.

4. Identity

Ethnic Make-up: Finn 93%, Swede 6%, Sami 0.11%, Roma 0.12%, Tatar 0.02%.
Religions: Evangelical Lutheran 89%, Russian Orthodox 1%, none 9%, other 1%.

Finland, along with Iceland, is Nordic rather than Scandinavian. This is reflected in their language, which is not Germanic in origin. While many social values are the same, there are subtle differences with Scandinavians.

Morocco

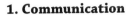

1. Communication

Languages: Classical Arabic is Morocco's official language, but the country's distinctive Arabic dialect is the most widely spoken language in Morocco. In addition, about 10 million Moroccans, mostly in rural areas, speak Berber - which exists in Morocco in three different dialects (Tarifit, Tashelhit, and Tamazight) - either as a first language or bilingually with the spoken Arabic dialect. French, which remains Morocco's unofficial third language, is taught universally and still serves as Morocco's primary language of commerce and economics; it is also widely used in education and government. Many Moroccans in the northern part of the country speak Spanish. English, while still far behind French and Spanish in terms of number of speakers, is rapidly becoming the foreign language of choice among educated youth. English is taught in all public schools from the fourth year on.

When Moroccans greet each other they take their time and converse about their families, friends, and other general topics. Handshakes are the customary greeting between individuals of the same sex. Handshakes may be somewhat weak according to western standards. Once a relationship has developed, it is common to kiss on both cheeks, starting with the left cheek while shaking hands, men with men and women with women. In any greeting that does take

place between men and women, the woman must extend her hand first. If she does not, a man should bow his head in greeting.

When entering a social function, it is correct to shake hands with the person to your right and then continue around the room going from right to left, and when leaving to say good-bye to each person individually.

Moroccans are non-confrontational. They may agree rather than cause anyone to lose face.

They expect a fair amount of haggling. Moroccans seldom see an offer as final. Decisions are made slowly - the process is as important as the outcome, and rushing it would be interpreted as an insult. Moroccans can be deliberate and forceful negotiators.

The society is extremely bureaucratic. Most decisions require several layers of approval. It may take several visits to accomplish simple tasks.

2. Life Values

The Concept of Shame - *Hshuma*: Moroccans' most cherished possession is their honour and dignity, which reflects not only on themselves but also on all members of their extended family.

Moroccans will go out of their way to preserve their personal honour. *Hshuma* occurs when other people know that they have behaved inappropriately.

A Moroccan's sense of self-worth is externally focused, so the way others see them is of paramount importance. If someone is shamed, they may be ostracized by society, or even worse, by their family. To avoid *hshuma*, many Moroccans will say or do things publicly because it makes them look good or helps them avoid embarrassment or awkwardness.

Moroccans judge people on appearances, so it is important for them to dress and present themselves well.

Conservative Moroccans may not entertain mixed-sex groups at a dinner in their home. Food is generally served at a knee-high round table. The guest of honour generally sits next to the host. A washing basin will be brought to the table before the meal is served. Each guest holds their hands over the basin while water is poured over them. The host will begin eating after he blesses the food, then everyone begins to eat.

Food is served from a communal bowl. Eating and drinking is done with the right hand only - food is scooped with a piece of bread or the thumb and first two fingers of the right hand. A person should never reach across the bowl to get something from the other side. Honoured guests will have choice cuts of meat put in front of them. Water is often served from a communal glass. The washing basin is brought around the table again at the end of the meal. Providing an abundance of food is a sign of hospitality. Mint tea is served when meeting someone, as this demonstrates hospitality.

3. Relationships

The family is the most significant unit of Moroccan life and plays an important role in all social relations. The individual is always subordinate to the family or group. Nepotism (favouritism) is viewed positively, since it indicates patronage of one's family. The family consists of both the nuclear and the extended family. The elderly are revered and respected and often exert a great influence on the rest of the family.

Moroccans prefer to do business with those they know and respect; therefore they expect to spend time cultivating a personal relationship before any business is conducted. Who you know is more important than what you know, so it is important in Morocco to network and cultivate a number of contacts who may then assist you in working your way through the serpentine bureaucracy.

4. Identity

Ethnic Make-up: Arab-Berber 99.1%, Jewish 0.2%, other 0.7%.

Religion: Islam is practised by the majority of Moroccans and governs their personal, political, economic and legal lives. Islam emanated from what is today Saudi Arabia. Among certain obligations for Muslims is to pray five times a day - at dawn, noon, afternoon, sunset, and evening. The exact time is listed in the local newspaper each day. Friday is the Muslim holy day. Everything is closed. Many companies also close on Thursday, making the weekend Thursday and Friday. During the holy month of Ramadan all Muslims must fast from dawn to dusk and are only permitted to work six hours per day. Fasting includes no eating, drinking, cigarette smoking, or gum chewing.

Expatriates are not required to fast; however, they must not eat, drink, smoke, or chew gum in public. Each night at sunset, families and friends gather together to celebrate the breaking of the fast (*iftar*). The festivities often continue well into the night. In general, things happen more slowly during Ramadan. Many businesses operate on a reduced schedule. Shops may be open and closed at unusual times.

? DISCUSSION POINTS

1. What are some of the things that a foreign visitor could unintentionally do that might annoy a Finnish person? What might be some of the things you would find difficult about living in Finland, or what things might you enjoy?

2. Which areas of life in Morocco do you think are not affected by Islam?

→ ACTIVITIES

1. Watch the following talk by Sheena Iyengar, where she discusses "Choice" and how cultural influences affect our choices:
http://www.ted.com/talks/sheena_iyengar_on_the_art_of_choosing.html

2. Choose one of the cultures in this tutorial and compare your own culture with it. Note any contrasts you see in each of the areas: *Communication, Life Values, Relationships* and *Identity*.

Adjusting to a new culture 1

OBJECTIVES OF THIS TUTORIAL

This tutorial focuses specifically on the process that people typically go through, during their initial period in a new cultural context. We will look at some different stages of cultural adjustment and the characteristics of those stages.

Introduction

Relocation into a new cultural situation is a huge step. The changes and contrasts in the simple things such as the language, food, television, weather, shopping and socialising are only a small part of the relocation process. It is often the deeper differences in customs, mentality, worldview and interpersonal interaction that have a more profound effect.

There are many different reactions and feelings people have, when faced with the challenges of moving and living for the long-term in an (initially) unfamiliar cultural context. Although it is often an exciting, interesting and positive time of learning, there will probably be days when it seems overwhelming and you feel that you just want to be back in your own culture, where you feel comfortable and can relax. No matter what kind of a person you are, or what preparation you have had previously, one of the major factors in adjustment is your *willingness* to make the adjustment, and your *motivation* to keep walking through those challenging times.

Your motivation is, of course, based on your overall *purpose* for being in the new culture and new situation in the first place. If you can find a deep and satisfying answer to the question, *Why am I (and my family) here?* then that will get you through the initial stages of culture adjustment better than anything else. If we are convinced that God is the one who has guided and led us to where we are for His purposes, then we will trust Him with the details of our living situation, new foods, new neighbours, and all the rest of the daily adjustments we must make - we will be more patient through the challenges of that process. Being more relaxed because we know He is in control can also help us to be open to see the fun side of cultural adjustment, and see it as a positive time, that will help in the process of us becoming more like Christ.

There are some distinct stages that have been recognised in people as they adjust to their host country, the host culture and their new daily activities. Looking at these stages can help us to recognize in ourselves that we will probably go through some similar feelings and attitudes, and hopefully we will be more prepared and objective about it at the time. No person's experience is exactly like another's, but you should be aware of some of the thoughts and feelings that you or your family *might* experience, during your initial adjustment to a new cultural living situation.

'Culture Shock'

'Culture shock' is a term you have probably heard and you may have an existing view of what it actually is. When people use it in reference to expatriate relocation it refers to the process of coming to understand and adapt to differences in culture through daily interaction and situations.

It is probably better to call it 'culture adjustment'. The term 'culture shock' can be misleading, because many people making a planned move to a new culture have had time to think about the move and prepare themselves in some way for it, so they won't face a sudden 'shock' that hits them out of the blue and that they have no control over. For most people, adjusting cross-culturally is a gradual process with a mix of 'positive' and 'negative' experiences, as they gradually adjust to a new set of rules for living, relating, communicating and doing just about everything else, and in effect, as they become a different person in the process.

Some of the factors that make cultural adjustment more difficult for some people, have

to do with their lack of preparation for another culture. If someone hasn't thought about it too much before, they will probably struggle to really *believe* in cultural differences and as a result, they will probably tend to impose their own cultural value system on others. This can lead them to think people who are behaving differently are behaving wrongly. They will tend to think that the way they behave themselves is natural and normal and the way other people behave, if it's different, is wrong or at the least, misguided. Generally, people who begin to think like this have had limited contact with people different from themselves and so have no experiential basis for believing in, and therefore understanding, the real scope of the differences that exist in other cultures.

Culture adjustment is a process that affects people of all different walks of life and ages; teachers, managers, sports people, business people, aid workers, medical personnel, children and teenagers all deal with some degree of adjustment as part of international relocation. Learning to recognise stages of the process of adjustment is helpful because it is important to realise it is a process that is common to everyone, and that we *can* work through it, and gradually become well adjusted to our new situation.

Common stages of adjustment

One way of describing the varying stages of culture adjustment that have been recognized is:

1. The Honeymoon - Initial Enthusiasm (First week or two in host country)

This is a period of initial enthusiasm and excitement, hope and stimulation. Everything is exotic and quaint. The attitude toward the host country is generally positive, mixed with enthusiasm for the move and the new things you are experiencing. Little is expected of you. Interaction with the host culture is primarily passive.

At this stage, you are probably unaware of most cultural differences. It may not occur to you that you may be making cultural mistakes or that you may be misinterpreting much of the behaviour going on around you. You have no reason not to trust your instincts.

2. Culture Fatigue - Initial realisation of the challenges of adjustment (After the first few weeks)

Wider exposure to the country and culture means more realistic and more mixed reactions. You are trying to establish daily life routines and even those can be a challenge to accomplish. Enthusiasm is tempered with frustration. Feelings of vulnerability and dependence are common. Homesickness is frequent. Nothing seems routine or has yet become 'easy' or 'fun'. Limited language ability undermines confidence. Close bonds can be formed with other expatriates rather than locals. The differences in behaviour combined with the stress of adapting to a new daily routine sometimes lead to criticism of the host culture. Symptoms of culture fatigue can start to appear such as boredom, lethargy, irritability and hostility toward the host culture.

You now realise that differences exist between the way you and the local people behave, though you understand very little about what these differences are, how numerous they might be, or how deep they might go. You know there's a problem here, but you're not sure about the size of it. You're not so sure of your instincts anymore, and you realise there are some things you don't understand. You may start to worry about how hard it's going to be to figure these people out.

3. Initial Adjustment (After the first six months or so)

Routines are re-established - you now know what to do to 'get by' and how to do what you need to. You are able to communicate in the language with people in a limited way. Some aspects of the country and culture now seem normal. Adjustment to the physical aspects of the host country is beginning to improve. You are somewhat more self-reliant. You are more positive about your ability to function. An understanding and empathy with the host culture starts to develop. You feel more comfortable with your routines and surroundings.

You know cultural differences exist, you know what some of these differences are, and you try to adjust your own behaviour accordingly. It doesn't come naturally yet - you have to make a conscious effort to behave in culturally appropriate ways, but you are much more aware of how your behaviour is coming across to the local people. You are in the process of replacing old instincts with new ones. You know now that you will be able to figure these people out if you can remain objective.

4. Further Adjustment - Enthusiasm (After the first year or more)

Your relocation is now a distant memory and your host country feels more like 'home'. The effects of culture adjustment lessen as a genuine enjoyment of the new location develops. Elements of the host culture's behaviours and values are adopted. You are less likely to criticise things that are different, and certain areas of the host culture are now preferred to the way you used to do things. You can communicate fairly well and have developed some relationships that are becoming closer and can sometimes even relax and enjoy socialising with local people, or having deeper, more open conversations with them.

You no longer have to think about what you're doing in order to do the 'right thing'. Culturally appropriate behaviour is now second nature to you; you can trust your instincts because they have been reconditioned by the new culture. It takes little effort now for you to be culturally sensitive.

The diagram below shows the typical "U" curve of cross-cultural adjustment:

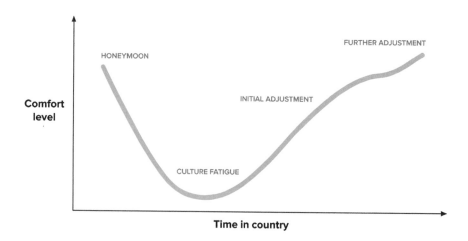

? DISCUSSION POINTS

1. Think back and remember a time when you have you felt out of your depth in a new situation - e.g. at a new job, a new group, a new school or university or a new country. Think about how you felt initially - what bothered you most? How did you learn to cope with it long term - did you recognize in yourself any of the characteristic stages of culture adjustment? How long did it take you to feel comfortable? What would you say was the most important factor in that process?

➡ ACTIVITIES

1. Watch as Yasmeen Islam describes her cultural adjustment to life in Australia - think about the stages of cultural adjustment she went through and what the things are that she remembers most about that time: http://youtu.be/cdMlK_JXGf0

2. Try to find a person who is a fairly recent immigrant to your country and ask them about their adjustment to the culture here. Can they tell you the story of what it was like when they first came to the country? What did they find difficult at first? How long did it take till they felt at home? What kinds of things did they find helpful as they adjusted to the culture and lifestyle here?

Adjusting to a new culture 2

OBJECTIVES OF THIS TUTORIAL

This tutorial looks at some practical ways that the adjustment to a new culture can be made easier. It looks at which attitudes and activities are the most helpful as people adjust to another context.

Introduction

There are many theories on making cultural adjustment easier, and a lot of resources that approach the challenge of adjustment from different points of view. However, most people agree that the very best way to adjust to a culture is to *learn* about it - familiarity, understanding and eventual adjustment come through knowing about your new context and getting to know local people.

Because of the particular goals you have to be in the context in the first place, your initial years will be spent in doing 'culture/language acquisition' activities. You will be working through a systematic program of learning to communicate, understanding the culture and getting to know the people around you - and this also happens to be the best way for you to adjust to your new country and culture as well. In the tutorials following this one, we will be looking at specific details in the process of culture/language acquisition. In this tutorial we are going to discuss some general principles of adjusting well to a new culture.

Prior to relocation

Before you move, it is important for individuals, couples and families to learn as much about their new host country as possible. Personal research should look at the people, culture, social norms, religions, language, food, entertainment, and accommodation - in fact anything you can find out about the country and its people. Good preparation can go a long way in helping you with your eventual adjustment to the culture.

As a goal for your personal research you should try to gain:

- An introduction to the country and its history, politics and culture.
- An understanding of the culture's values, customs and etiquette and their possible impact on work and social life.
- An understanding of the possible lifestyle realities in the destination region.
- An initial connection to the other team members working in the area.
- An introduction to the languages and cultures in that region and specific characteristics of those.

Attitudes that help when adjusting to a new culture

Culture adjustment is something everyone experiences to one degree or another. For everyone there will be times of stress and fatigue and even the feeling of being out of control of your environment. No matter how well we prepare for our destination, there will be times when we just want to be in a familiar place where we understand what is going on and can function and communicate freely.

The challenge of culture adjustment could be said to be one of the major reasons that there are still unreached peoples in the world - it is where the 'rubber hits the road' for the Church in its efforts to fulfill the Great Commission. Because it isn't in a sense the big decision to *go* that is as significant as the daily decisions people make to *stay*. One thing we do know is that the Lord understands and appreciates the sacrifice His people make in putting themselves into difficult situations - or even just out of their comfort zone - for the sake of His purposes in the lives of others. One of the most helpful attitudes to have when facing culture fatigue or stress is to remember what the Lord Jesus Christ did for us.

There are other attitudes also that will help you to bridge cultures:

Realise that everyone experiences culture fatigue. Find someone who has gone through culture adjustment and has a positive attitude now. Get perspective. Avoid others who are in a permanent state of complaining and culture shock (unless you feel you can help them).

Admit that you don't know. Knowing that we don't know everything, that a situation does not make sense, that our assumptions may be wrong, is part of the process of becoming culturally aware. Assume first that you might be misunderstanding the situation and be ready to learn from it: there are different ways of doing things, not worse, not better.

Suspend judgements. Collect as much information as possible so you can describe the situation accurately before evaluating it. Begin looking for logical reasons behind everything that seems strange, confusing, difficult or threatening. Assume that other people are as resourceful as we are and that their way will add to what we know. They have probably found perfectly good, but different, solutions to the same problems we face.

Empathy. In order to understand another person, we need to try standing in their shoes. Through empathy we learn how other people would like to be treated by us. Try to think about the other person's point of view.

Systematically check your assumptions. Ask your local friends or neighbours for feedback and constantly check your assumptions to make sure that you clearly understand the situation.

Become comfortable with ambiguity. The more complicated and uncertain life is, the more we tend to seek control and to work everything out. Learn to recognize this in yourself and allow the Lord to be the One who is in control - guiding and leading in each situation you face.

Celebrate diversity. Find ways of sharing and appreciating the culture around you and your local friends and co-workers, and also the diverse cultures of your expat friends and co-workers. Find ways to talk about differences or similarities in a positive and appreciative way. Relax your grip on your own culture.

Enjoy your situation. Make a list of all the positive things you can identify about your present situation. List all the things you enjoy or appreciate about the culture around you, and the things that you are looking forward to finding out more about, or to trying for yourself.

Maintain a healthy sense of humour. There are often a lot of funny situations that happen when you are adjusting to a new culture and learning a new language - learning to laugh at yourself and your mistakes and to talk about them with others can be a great stress reliever.

Have faith. Remember that the Lord is with you and you will work through culture adjustment to brighter days ahead.

Think about the needs of others. Be concerned about others and you will be less worried about how you feel.

Activities that help with cultural adjustment

Learn the Language and Culture. As we said before, this is going to be an ongoing process for you perhaps for several years - it is good to remember that it is helping you to adjust and feel more comfortable the more you learn.

Explore! Get a sense for the physical environment, look for parks, sports facilities, bus stops, etc. Get an initial sense for how people greet each other, wait in line, etc. Find out where people meet and socialise. Make an effort to go to those places.

Use local media: In every country, a lot about the culture is revealed by the media, which includes: books/poetry, newspapers, magazines, radio, television, movies/theater, songs and music. Your ability to use the media to learn about the culture depends on how well you speak and read the language, but this will increase with time.

Adjust your schedule. Try to fit into a rhythm of life in your host culture. Adjust to their time schedule for meals and work.

Keep busy. Keep active. Keep your mind occupied. Don't sit around and feel sorry for yourself.

Join In. Begin to find the things that local people do and take part in those things. Find ways to actively participate, to become involved in the life of your community and its people. Much of this involvement happens automatically as you go about living and working in your village or city, but you can also make a conscious effort to become involved in community activities outside your work and meet people you ordinarily would not.

Take care of yourself. Make sure you are exercising, getting enough sleep, eating properly, and doing things you enjoy. Draw on your personal resources for handling stress. You've done it many times before, and you can do it again.

Keep in touch. Connect with friends and family at home.

Keep a journal. This will help you make sense out of what you are feeling, how you have changed, and what you have gained so far from your time in your new country. It helps to share this with family and friends, to share your experiences with them.

Make friends. Getting to know sympathetic locals - those who are willing to help you initially - is a great comfort and a way to begin to develop deeper relationships. Ask people for help in learning to do the basic things and you will find the people who want to get to know you. Share with them some of the challenges of your adjustment to this new situation.

? DISCUSSION POINTS

1. Think about the activities that you like to do now that help you to enjoy life and relax. E.g., exercise, watch movies, shop, cook, fish, bike ride, read, walk, go out to eat, etc. Which of these do you think you will probably be able to continue to do in a new cultural situation? Which activities might you not be able to do and how do you feel about that?

6.11 Becoming equipped to communicate 1

OBJECTIVES OF THIS TUTORIAL

This tutorial introduces a practical program for culture and language acquisition, called *Becoming Equipped to Communicate*. We will look at some of the underlying principles, and the first part of the program. There are also some practical exercises to do in your community.

Introduction

As we discussed earlier (tutorials 4.16 - 4.21), there are many different kinds of language learning programs and courses, but, because we have specific goals in mind for the outcome of our learning, we need a specific program that is suited to those goals. *Becoming Equipped to Communicate (BEC)* has been designed with our specific long-term goals in mind. It is a relationship-centred program that takes people to a high level of proficiency in culture and language, while encouraging the development of friendships as an integral part of the learning process.

We are going to use the *BEC* guide as a reference for our next set of tutorials, so you should download it now (from accesstruth.com) and have it available for reading and reference. You will also do some practical exercises and activities based on the *BEC* during these next weeks.

Getting Started

Read: *BEC* Preface and Pages 9-12

Page 9 of BEC includes a description of the underlying principles that shaped the program and how it works:

- *Relationship-centered*
- *Culture-derived*
- *Experience-oriented*
- *Comprehension-based*
- *Communication-focused*
- *Proficiency-measured*

These principles are generally accepted as being the most effective ways to learn language and understand culture. Once you have finished your reading, look again at the list of principles above and try to describe what each one means in your own words (no need to write anything, just think it through).

? DISCUSSION POINTS

1. Imagine that a new person who has just moved into your neighbourhood from overseas has asked you for help in settling in - what are the first things you would help them with, or the places you would show them in your local community?

2. If your new neighbour asked you to help them with some "survival phrases" (BEC p11), which are the ones you think would be most useful that you would help them to learn? Make a list of things they might need to say just to get around and meet more people.

3. Now imagine you are a new person in your community who has just arrived from overseas with very little ability in the language. Who are the people you would ask for help in settling in, how would you go about it and what would you ask them to help you with? Do you think people would go out of their way to be helpful to you? Why or why not?

➡ ACTIVITIES

1. The following activity is adapted from the *Investigate Your New Neighborhood* activity on the website http://www.lifelearner.org/culture. Take a small notebook or recording device and record answers to the following questions as you walk around your local neighbourhood.

What do you see out your front door?

A road? Fields? Mountains? Another house? A highway?

Does your house have a front yard? What is it like? Is it similar or different to your neighbours'?

Take a walk around your neighbourhood

Is your neighbourhood residential? Commercial? A combination of the two?

How would you describe the types of buildings? Apartment buildings, homes, store fronts?

Do any particular buildings seem to stand out? If so, why?

How far do you have to walk to: 1) a place to buy food - supermarket, local shop 2) to a church 3) to the next-door neighbour's house 4) to a recreation area or park.

Are there trees, flowers along the streets? In peoples' yards?

Do you have to walk on the street? Or is there a walkway of some kind?

Are others outside walking? Are there animals around? Are children playing outside?

What activities can you see taking place, and who is doing them?

Try to meet and talk to one or more local people that you haven't spoken to before - be friendly and introduce yourself.

When you return home

Make a rudimentary map of your neighbourhood and label the buildings and streets as far as you can.

6.12 Becoming equipped to communicate 2

OBJECTIVES OF THIS TUTORIAL

This tutorial continues to look at the *Becoming Equipped to Communicate* program, specifically:
Level 1: Relating through the Common and Familiar. We will introduce and practice the first two learning activities - *Participant Observation*, and *Listen and Act (listening comprehension).*

Introduction

Read: *BEC* Preface and Pages 13-18

Pages 13 to 15 explain some of the principles in setting up a routine for yourself as you begin to learn. *BEC* is not like most language programs where you go to a class and then go back to the rest of your life once class is over. It is designed to make the most of your normal life activities - including work, social activities and other things that you enjoy doing - so that they are all part of the learning experience. In a new cultural setting, these kinds of activities will take time and planning to become established, and eventually to become a routine part of your life. It is important to plan and think carefully from the beginning as your routine develops because it has a profound effect on how you will learn.

Page 16 describes the four different levels of the program - each level is designed to build on the skills and abilities learned in the level before, in the areas of language, culture and depth of relationships.

The note that page 18 touches on an important learning principle; *listen first, speak later*. This is something that doesn't come naturally to people learning a language, because most of us want to try say the words we are hearing straight away. It is generally agreed that people who are able to listen much more than they speak in the beginning stages of learning, have a much better chance of learning the natural intonation and pronunciation of the language, and that listening builds a solid foundation for speaking later on. As you will see, the first Level 1 activities do not require you to speak at all - only to listen.

Level 1: Relating through the Common and Familiar

Read: *BEC* Pages 19-26

These pages give an introduction to the three learning activities used during level 1:

- Participant Observation,
- Listen and Act (listening comprehension),
- Listen and Act (listening comprehension and speaking).

In the assignment for this tutorial you will try both a Participant Observation exercise (Learning activity 1), and a Listen and Act exercise (Learning activity 2).

If you look a the time schedule on page 25, you will see that most of your time during this early part of Level 1 is spent in Participant Observation exercises. Participant Observation is not just for the beginning stages of learning, it is something you will continue to do throughout your whole learning time, but what is it?

Participant Observation

Basically, Participant Observation is learning to relate to others by experiencing their everyday lives with them in culturally appropriate ways. Sometimes it is described in more "scientific" terms by anthropologists:

- DeMUNCK and SOBO (1998) describe participant observation as "the primary method used by anthropologists doing fieldwork".
- "Participant observation is the process enabling researchers to learn about the activities of the people under study in the natural setting through observing and participating in those activities". (DeWALT & DeWALT, 2002).
- SCHENSUL, SCHENSUL, and LeCOMPTE (1999) define participant observation as "the process of learning through exposure to or involvement in the day-to-day or routine activities of participants in the researcher setting".

The major difference in the way we would define participant observation in comparison to the anthropologists' definitions above, relates to the differences in the way we see ourselves in the setting. We don't consider ourselves "researchers" doing an academic "study" of a culture or group of people. Our goal, on the other hand, is to become insiders in the culture and community, to get to know people and to develop real and close relationships with individuals there - to grow to understand what people think and how they feel from their perspective - to see through their eyes.

Participant Observation during Level 1 is simply joining in, or just being there, with people when they are doing the normal activities of life. Showing an interest in them and their lives and letting them know that you want to learn their language and culture by being a part of the things they are doing. This is easier in the beginning if you find one or two people who are willing to have you accompany them as they do various activities - shopping, leisure activities, visits, sports, work, family times, visit their home, paying bills, getting their car fixed, going to a wedding or funeral - then you can gradually meet more people through them.

So, Participant Observation is as much about you getting to know people and interacting with them, as it is about gathering language and cultural material from an objective point of view. But, you do have to be intentional in the situation, not just cruise along, but be purposefully observing, listening, jotting down questions or notes, and responding to the people there as you are able to.

Listen and Act

The Listen and Act learning activities used in Level 1 are based on a learning method called 'TPR' (Total Physical Response). TPR was developed by an American professor, James Asher, and is the combination of language and physical movement. A language helper or tutor gives commands in the target language, and learners respond with physical actions - like pointing, or doing the action ("Point to the basket", "Put the cup on the table", "Stand up", etc.). It is a very effective way of learning to hear and understand basic vocabulary for objects and actions, and then later to be able to use these yourself.

You can see Asher explaining TPR and some students using it to learn Spanish here: http://youtu.be/ikZY6XpB214 or see some African students using it to learn action words here: http://youtu.be/VHpdAxAVszE.

Read: *BEC* Pages 20-28

These pages give some more detail about Participant Observation, and also have the first learning plan for Level 1.

➡ ACTIVITIES

1. The following activity is adapted from the website http://www.lifelearner.org/culture, *Activities In The Neighbourhood*. This activity will help you to observe what people are doing in your local neighbourhood or town. As you do this activity, follow the first instruction in BEC Daily Learning Plan 1, Participant Observation and *observe, listen, respond* and *note*. Try to engage people in conversation, even if it is only greeting or asking a simple question - see what happens!

Take a walk down the street and take note of what you see people doing (children going to school or playing, women shopping, someone cleaning the street, people going to work or sitting in the sunshine, shopkeepers at work, tradesmen doing their work, etc.) Take pictures if appropriate.

Where are the activities taking place? In or by a home? In an office? In a store? On the street?

Who is doing each particular activity? Is it being done by a recognized tradesman (e.g., mechanic, painter, silversmith), by either a man or woman? Is it limited to a specific area (e.g., industrial area, shopping area), or to a certain season (grass cutting, fishing, shovelling snow)?

Is the activity essentially individual or cooperative? If the latter, who does what? Is food or payment provided for workers or helpers? Try to join in one or another of the activities and tell about your experience. Note the people's reaction and their instructions to you.

2. Watch the video (available on the accesstruth.com website) on Learning Activities that includes some demonstrations of *Participant Observation* and *Listen and Act* activities.

3. Find anyone you know - family, friend, neighbor - who speaks another language that you do not know (it doesn't have to be their first language, but they must speak it fairly well). Ask if they would help you with a learning exercise - it should take about two hours of their time. The exercise is from the Listen and Act exercise from Daily Learning Plan 1. You will try to learn to comprehend the words for the common types of people - woman, man, boy, girl, baby, old woman, old man, young woman, young man, etc. - in your helper's language. A page with photos is included for you to print out at the end of this tutorial - cut out the pictures so you can show each one separately to your helper.

Follow the instructions carefully - remember that your helper should say the words in a sentence, not just the words on their own, and they will need to repeat them many times until you are able to point to them correctly toward the end of the exercise. Relax, because you don't have to say anything, just listen to comprehend. Have fun!

I. Listen - start with two of the photos in front of you and the helper (choose the baby and the man in the suit). Point to the first photo and have your helper say (in his language) the name of the type of person in a sentence, such as *"This is a baby"*.

II. You will listen, but do not repeat what your helper says. Point to the next photo of the man and ask your helper to say it in a sentence, as he did the first time. *"This is a man."* (For this exercise it will be easier for you if he uses the same form of sentence for each photo - "This is a _____")

III. Then your helper can begin to randomly say the sentences for the two photos present, "*This is a man*," and you try to point to the picture of the man. Or, "*This is a baby*," and you try to point to the picture of the baby. Listen for the differences in the sentences - this is the part you are learning to comprehend, and relate to the picture of the person.

IV. Once you succeed in pointing correctly to those two first people, you can add a third, then a fourth, and on up till all nine photos are in front of you. Your helper should attempt to go through the items as randomly and unpredictably as possible to maximise your learning. He probably won't realise that you need to hear these things many, many times in order to understand them well. So don't become bored or move on too quickly! Have him continue as long as you need to, before adding another new photo (this can be around 30 times for each picture). Let him decide what each person would be called in his language, don't tell him what to say. If it turns out that two people would be called the same thing (e.g., if there is no distinction between little girl and teenage girl for instance) then just use one of the pictures.

V. Finally, when you can point correctly to all the types of people when he says the sentences, make a recording of him saying all the sentences so you can review it on your own later.

4. As an additional exercise, you can repeat the steps above, but have your helper say *different* sentences for each photograph, using the same 'people' words (man, woman, baby, etc.) but using a sentence referring to what each person is doing - "the baby is holding the brush", "the girl is jumping", "the man is using his phone", "the old man is reading", etc. You might still be able to recognise the words for the various people in these different sentences (depending on the language) and point to the correct one - try it and see how you go.

Becoming equipped to communicate 3

OBJECTIVES OF THIS TUTORIAL

This tutorial continues to look at the *Becoming Equipped to Communicate* program. We will look at another learning activity used during Level 1 - *Listen and Act with Speaking*. Then, we will move on to looking at the program for *Level 2: Relating through Daily Routines*.

Introduction

In the last tutorial we introduced the *Listen and Act* activity for listening comprehension. This activity is used right through Level 1 so that you learn to comprehend quite a number of words before you use them in speaking. Look quickly through the first 25 daily learning plans of Level 1 now, to see the type of vocabulary you will learn initially - remember, you will not be learning to *say* all of these things during these activities, but just to *hear and understand* them:

Scan: *BEC Pages 29-64*

After these first 25 learning plans, the program adds a new learning activity: *Listen and Act with Speaking*. Read the introduction to this activity:

Read: *BEC Page 65*

Listen and Act with Speaking

This new activity builds upon the foundation of the things you will have already learned up to this point: you will already be able to hear and understand quite a number of common vocabulary items. Now you will be ready to learn to say those things yourself. Once you can comprehend a word or phrase, and you have heard it repeated by a native speaker many times, it will be much easier for you to learn to say it correctly yourself. This follows a natural process of learning language: hear it → understand what it means → learn to say it → learn to use it correctly in context.

During the second half of Level 1 (daily learning plans 26-50) you will start to use the *Listen and Act with Speaking* learning exercise. You will also keep using *Participant Observation* and the *Listen and Act* learning exercise (for new vocabulary items that you have not heard before).

Look quickly through the next set of daily learning plans in Level 1 now (daily learning plans 26-50) to see basically what they cover:

Scan: *BEC* Pages 66-113

What will you learn during Level 1?

On pages 114 - 118 of the BEC is a 'Self-evaluation for Level 1'. A learner who has completed all the daily learning plans for Level 1 should be able to fill out the self-evaluation by answering either 'adequately well' or 'extremely well' to each question. Read through the Self-evaluation to get an idea of the type of language someone should be able to use at the end of Level 1.

Read: *BEC* Pages 114-118

By the end of Level 1, a learner will have also spent around 200 hours doing *Participant Observation* in the community - taking part in, and observing community activities with people. They will also have spent around 300 hours doing *Listen and Act* activities with a number of local people who have been willing to spend regular time with them. If you imagine yourself in this situation, it is a lot of potential time to have begun to develop some relationships with a variety of people in the community, and for local people to start to get to know you. You will also be starting to get an idea of how things work - the polite ways to greet people, the interesting places to visit, the things that are important to people, who your neighbours are, and the common activities in the community. You will begin to understand what it means to people for you to show an interest in them and to take the time to learn their language.

Level 2: Relating through Daily Routines

Read: *BEC* Pages 119-120

These pages give an introduction to the learning activities used during Level 2:

- Participant Observation,
- Working with Daily Routines.

Participant Observation continues to be a foundational part of the learning process - it is the time when you will be in real-life situations with people in the community, and in a sense it is where all of your learning comes together and solidifies into real functional ability. This is the time when your language and culture learning will be put into the pressure-cooker of life - and it is an essential part of the whole learning process. In the time schedule for Level 2 learners, on page 120 of the BEC, you will see that most of your time during this stage is spent in *Participant Observation* and the *Working with Daily Routines* activities.

? DISCUSSION POINTS

1. Imagine that a group of people from another country moved into a house near yours on your street. What is some of the information you would like to find out about them, and why they were here? What are some of the things that they could do to make you:

    a) feel suspicious or uneasy about them, or,

    b) feel reassured about having them as neighbours?

→ ACTIVITIES

1. Read the write-up called *Community Sketch* (available for download on the accesstruth.com website). Once you have read it, do the following exercises for your current community setting:

Develop your own community sketch for the major areas of community life.

Follow the suggestions in the write-up to develop a list of general activities for each area, and then list some specific activities for each area that you would be able to take part in if you were doing language and culture learning in your current community setting.

6.14 Becoming equipped to communicate 4

OBJECTIVES OF THIS TUTORIAL

This tutorial continues to look at the *Becoming Equipped to Communicate* program. We will do an exercise related to *Level 2: Relating through Daily Routines*.

Introduction

In the last tutorial you completed an exercise to develop a sketch or plan of your community, hopefully gaining a better picture of the major areas of the life of the community around you, and some of the activities related to those areas.

Participant Observation is still going to be a major part of Level 2 learning, but in this tutorial we will look at another learning activity used during Level 2 - *Working with daily routines*.

Working with Daily Routines

Read: *BEC* Pages 121-127

This activity is specifically designed for people at this early stage of language and culture learning, because it helps them to learn simple sentences and questions in the framework of common cultural situations. By focusing on the common daily routine activities of the people around them, they will be learning the language they need to be able to talk about those common activities with friends and neighbours. They will also begin to understand the kinds of things that people are involved in every day - which will be a perfect way to begin to build relationships with people, even though their language ability is still limited.

The Sample Daily Learning Plan for Level 2 that begins on page 123 describes the basic activities of a Level 2 learner. Read it through carefully. A learner will take part in, and use as a basis for learning, a series of Daily Routine activities from the life of the community around them. They will:

- identify the activities that are most common in the lives of people around them,
- learn to understand the descriptions and processes of those routine activities,
- and learn to understand common questions that might be asked about them.

During the second half of Level 2, they will go back and re-experience the same activities, with a much greater 'toolbox' of understanding and linguistic ability, so they will be able to engage in those same activities in a more natural way.

Many learners have found video to be a useful tool for Level 2 - you can read the procedure for making and using videos during the *Working with Daily Routines* activity beginning on page 128. There are some examples of videos learners have made available for you to view on the website.

Read: *BEC* Pages 128-138

What will you learn during Level 2?

On pages 139-147 of the BEC is a 'Self-evaluation for Level 2'. A learner who has completed all of the daily learning plans for Level 2 should be able to fill out the self-evaluation by answering either 'adequately well' or 'extremely well' to each question. Read through the Self-evaluation to get an idea of the type of language someone should be able to use and the cultural understanding they will have at the end of Level 2.

Scan: *BEC* Pages 139-147

By the end of Level 2, a learner will have also spent many hours doing *Participant Observation* in the community - taking part in, and observing community activities with people. They will also have spent many hours doing daily routine activities with a number of local people who have been willing to spend regular time with them and have them share in some of their daily activities in order for them to learn. They will be able to function in the community in culturally appropriate ways in the general activities of daily life, and talk about those things and ask simple questions.

The daily routine activities in Level 2 are an ideal way to have an "excuse" to spend time with people, and have them talk about the things that they do every day. By the end of Level 2, a learner should have some local people who are interested in being friends with them, who want to help them to settle in to the community and see them continue to learn. They should have a fairly well established routine of regular activities and people that they regularly spend time with, building a good foundation for the next level of learning, and for establishing deeper relationships.

? DISCUSSION POINTS

1. Discuss with friends or family your 'community sketch' and the ideas for activities that you came up with for the last tutorial. See if they have any other ideas for major areas or activities they think are important in the community that you might have missed, that a learner would want to experience and explore to gain a broad understanding of life and culture in your community.

➡ ACTIVITIES

1. On the website you can view examples of videos learners in Thailand made as they were working through Level 2 - have a look at these videos if you haven't already.

2. Choose one of the activities from your 'community sketch' you did for the last tutorial that would be suitable for Level 2 learning, and apply the *Working with Daily Routines* learning activity to it. You can use a friend or family member as your language helper to describe the setting, and the process involved. Make a simple video or set of photos, and then have your helper make a recording of the description, and the steps of the process in English.

3. Further activity: If you have access to a member of another language and culture community, do the same exercise as the one above, but use their language instead of English, and preferably use an activity that is culturally appropriate to them (such as making a meal from their country, or playing a game from their home culture).

Becoming equipped to communicate 5

OBJECTIVES OF THIS TUTORIAL

This tutorial continues to look at the *Becoming Equipped to Communicate* program, focusing on *Level 3: Relating through Sharing Life Stories*.

Introduction

In this tutorial we will look at the next stage of the BEC program, Level 3. At this level, learners are moving from being involved only in the outward behaviour of people, to beginning to try to see and understand the underlying motivations for people's actions, what they appreciate and prioritise in life and what their beliefs are about.

Level 3: Relating through Sharing Life Stories

Read: *BEC* Pages 149-161

These pages give an introduction to the learning activities used during level 3:

- Participant Observation,
- Sharing Life Stories.

Participant Observation continues to be a part of the learning process during Level 3, but less time is spent on it during this stage. Because learners at Level 3 have already spent many hours participating in activities in the community, they should now be looking for new things to do that they have not taken part in before, so that they can continue to learn and broaden their understanding, and ability to engage in community life.

Sharing life stories

This new activity is based on the increased cultural and linguistic ability of a learner at Level 3. They are now able to relate culturally with people and to talk about more complex things with them, using sentences and questions. This allows them to participate with people on a deeper level, and the *Sharing Life Stories* activity gives them a helpful framework to do that and to continue learning at the same time. The focus during the first part of Level 3 is on hearing stories from local people and learning to understand them. During the second half of Level 3, the learner will tell life stories themselves, both from their own experience and also experiences they have heard told to them by others. This stage follows a natural progression in the learning process, culturally, linguistically and relationally.

Language and culture helpers

You will notice that the time schedule for Level 3 includes four hours per day in the Sharing Life Stories activity. The BEC (p159-160) says, *"This is because at this point in your learning, you want to spend most of your time listening to others as they share stories with you about their lives. But, four hours is a lot of time each day. It is unreasonable to expect that you will be able to spend four hours with a single person every day in your Sharing Life Stories learning exercise. You should try to include lots of others in helping you to learn at this level. This is a great way to get to know them. The daily learning plans for Level 3 will be divided into parts to help you involve more than one person each day."*

This point is a key one that sometimes gets lost in practice when learners are in a cross-cultural situation. It isn't a simple task to find people in the community with regular time to spend with you, and it is something you will have to actively and continually pursue in order to see it happen. There are often people in the community who *do* have time on their hands and would be very happy to have someone sit and spend time with them and listen to their life stories; older retired people, bored shopkeepers, mothers at a play group, a work mate or colleague, a neighbour during their recreational time, someone wanting to learn some English as an exchange, a person you are helping with garden work or voluntary work, people in hospital, etc. - if you think actively and creatively you will find people to spend time with. The key is to keep challenging yourself and don't settle for one language helper or tutor as your main conversation partner.

Read: *BEC* Pages 185-186

Look at the Self-evaluation for Level 3 (page 185) noting the numbers of people mentioned in the questions that the learner must have spent time with, hearing and telling life stories. This feature of getting to know and spending time with a number of people in the community is an integral part of the program, based on the eventual goal of speaking into that community with truth.

? DISCUSSION POINTS

1. Imagine you are a Level 3 learner in your own community. Think of some areas of community life that you have never taken part in that would be "gaps" in your understanding if you were trying to understand fully the culture and life of the people in your community.

2. Are there some cultural areas and activities in your community that you would not want to take part in or even to observe? Do you think you would find out about those kinds of activities in a cross-cultural situation, and if so, how?

→ ACTIVITIES

1. Watch this video of Mark Driscoll discussing cultural immersion: http://youtu.be/RLbpDV7gmV8

2. Watch this video of Sardool Singh's story of his migration to Australia: http://youtu.be/jw7cS7oZZww As he speaks, take note of any of the following:

- The main facts and details that he shares from his life.
- Unusual situations in his life that you would return to later if you had a chance to speak to him again:
- Exciting, difficult, memorable, or life changing events.
- Experiences that he has had that seem unique to him.
- Complicated situations that took him by surprise.
- Parts of the story that are really confusing to you that you might clarify later.
- Any questions that you have about his life that you would return to with follow up questions later.

3. The activity below is adapted from the website http://www.lifelearner.org/culture, *Recreation And Leisure Activities*. This activity will help you to learn more about recreation in your local neighbourhood or town by taking part in a recreational activity.

Your goal for this activity is to get into a situation where you are a participant observer in some community activity related to recreation and leisure. This might mean attending a sporting event, a social event, getting into a conversation with someone engaged in a leisure activity, or finding out more about a club or group in your area by talking to its members. As you take part in the activity, follow the instructions for Participant Observation and *observe, listen, respond* and *note*.

Engage with people and be a part of what they are doing, listening to how they talk and being interested in what interests them. Remember, participant observation is not a detached research activity, but it is an engagement with the activity and the people in a real way. Try to enjoy yourself. Note anything you learn or observe, and gather any research, notes, photos or recordings from the activity.

Below are some of the things you could eventually come to understand about this area by taking part in recreational activities and talking to people about them. You shouldn't go into this activity thinking that you have to answer all of the questions below, these are simply an example of some of the things you would eventually learn about recreation activities in a community if you continued to be a participant observer over a long period of time.

- During which times of the day do people have more leisure? During which times of the year? What do people do in their leisure time? Do they sing, carve, sew, visit, tell stories, travel, go to a movie, watch TV, gamble, etc.? How much time is taken up with these activities? Are they done individually or as a group?

- What do people do when they go to town or to the main shopping or recreation areas? Do people eat out, and if so, how often would they do this? Are there places to just sit and talk? Are there parks and do many people enjoy them? What kind of facilities are available in public places (entertainment, rest rooms, eating)?

- What games do children play? Are any similar to ones played in your own country? What toys do children have? Who makes the toys? Or are they bought commercially? Sketch and describe the production and use of one or more local toys.

- Do adults play games? If so, what and when? What kind of clothing is worn? by men? by women? Is this only appropriate for games and sports? Are any sports gender specific? Is this changing?

- Do any games have a ritualistic significance? Are any used in courting? during the wedding activities? What games do adults play with children? Are these just for amusement, or for teaching?

- What sports are played? By whom? Are these played by people in the neighborhood or only by professionals? Are uniforms worn? Are certain sports played at particular times of the year? What is the general interest level for partici-pation? for cheering?

- What amusements have been introduced as a result of contact with outsiders? Do people enjoy learning a new game? Describe the rules for playing one or more games.
- In which recreational activities would it be appropriate for you to participate? What linguistic or physical skills do you need to develop in order to participate acceptably? How do people try to teach you the rules for participating?

Becoming equipped to communicate 6

OBJECTIVES OF THIS TUTORIAL

This tutorial continues to look at the *Becoming Equipped to Communicate* program, focusing on the last stage of learning, *Level 4: Relating through Lifeview Conversation.*

Introduction

In this tutorial we will look at the last stage of the BEC program, Level 4. During this stage, learners will start to understand and talk about the beliefs that motivate the behaviour of people around them. They will be able to understand the opinions of others, as well as support their own opinions. They will learn to talk about the bigger issues in the world, and find ways to talk about concepts that are new to them but that they want to describe.

Level 4: Relating through Lifeview Conversation

Read: *BEC* Pages 187-188

Your proficiency goal for this level

On page 187 is a detailed description of the level you can expect to reach in your language ability and cultural understanding by the end of Level 4. Hopefully as you read that description you can imagine yourself at that place - where you feel a part of the community and can interact fairly naturally with people around you. It will be a lot of work to get there, but it *is* possible; many people have made that effort and have become functional members of a new community. It is an exciting privilege to have the opportunity to come from the outside and to gradually become an 'insider' into another culture and group of people. It is something that will change you and your perspective on the world around you forever.

The Four Life Perspectives

Read: *BEC* Pages 189-198

The main learning activity used during Level 4 is *Lifeview Conversation*. The conversations you will have with local people during this last stage of your learning program will be based on the outline introduced during Level 3 of the BEC - Four Life Perspectives, but it will be expanded to cover a lot more detail during Level 4.

On page 189 the BEC says:

> "In your Level 4 exercises, you will further explore these four life perspectives as you talk with community members. You want to know what people actually describe as their motivation for behaviour in the community. What do people appreciate and prioritise in their lives? What are their underlying beliefs about life? How do the beliefs that people claim actually measure up to what they typically do?."

These kinds of insights are so important because as you look forward to communicating God's Truth with this group of people at a LATER date, you need to FIRST understand the ways that their thinking about life will be impacted by the Truth that you want to share with them. You want to later apply God's Truth to their lives in ways that are relevant to them, but with an awareness of what correct and incorrect beliefs about life you are confronting in the process.

So, Level 4 activities are related directly to the overall goal you have: speaking into people's lives with Truth. The Message that you came to bring has to cross the bridge of their culture and language and be engaging and relevant to them as they hear it. YOU must become that bridge and Level 4 exercises will make you more effective in that role. Even if you are not in a major teaching role, your life and conversation will still communicate. As you spend time in conversations on a number of relevant topics with a variety of people during Level 4, you will be gaining proficiency in language ability, and also learning a huge amount culturally about they ways people think and how they communicate those thoughts.

Lifeview Conversation

Read: *BEC* Pages 199-206

As you saw from the description of the *Lifeview Conversation* learning exercise, conversations of this kind are not just 'chitchat' or 'shooting the breeze'. They require thought and planning beforehand:

- finding people to talk with,
- planning a group of topics to cover during your conversation,
- developing good questions to ask for each topic,
- thinking carefully about cultural and relational issues for the particular person you will be speaking with,
- and following the correct procedure.

This takes practice! On page 201, *BEC* says *"You should practice the steps in your own language with people from your own community so that you have the process well in mind before you try in a second language."*

In the activity for this tutorial you will review the process by carefully reading the instructions for how to conduct the *Lifeview Conversation* activity, and you will plan topics and questions for a lifeview conversation. For the next two tutorials you will have a conversation with two different people you know in your own community so you can practice the technique.

➡ ACTIVITIES

1. Read the instructions again on pages 199 - 206 of the *BEC*. Prepare for one lifeview conversation, which you will have with two different people sometime over the next few weeks (these conversations will be the activity for the two tutorials following this one).

- Think of two people you know well, that you could have a conversation with - these can be family members or friends - your main goal is to practice the conversation technique.

- Choose three topics with questions that would be appropriate to discuss with these two people. There are many examples of topics with questions given on pages 214- 294 of *BEC* - you can use these and adapt them to your culture and the people you have in mind.

- Write out your topics and questions, following the steps of how the conversation should go, to remind yourself as you guide the conversation. (Simplified instructions are below for you to follow)

- Plan to get together with your two friends - one at a time, and for around two hours for each person.

- Get a recording device ready, so you can practice recording the conversation.

6.17 Becoming equipped to communicate 7

This tutorial continues to look at the *Becoming Equipped to Communicate* program, focusing again on the last stage of learning, *Level 4: Relating through Lifeview Conversation*. For this tutorial, we will be practising the *Lifeview Conversation* learning activity.

What will you learn in Level 4?

Read: *BEC* Pages 296-307

Read through the Self-evaluation for Level 4, noting the types of topics and the level of understanding reached at the end of this stage of learning.

➡ ACTIVITIES

1. Meet with one of the people you planned to have a conversation with and do the Lifeview Conversation activity with them, following your notes and using the technique you reviewed in the last tutorial. Remember this is your first try... and things almost never go to plan.

2. Listen to the recording you made of the conversation. While you listen, make notes of any further questions that you would like to ask if you had another conversation with this person, and any interesting observations that you've made. Reflect on the four life perspectives and note anything from the conversation that lends support to, or serves as an example for, any of the perspectives.

6.18 Becoming equipped to communicate 8

OBJECTIVES OF THIS TUTORIAL

This tutorial gives a summary overview of the *Becoming Equipped to Communicate* program. For this tutorial, we will again be practising the *Lifeview Conversation* learning activity.

Introduction

Now that we have finished looking at the detail of the *BEC* program, we will give a summary overview of the whole program - the four stages and the learning exercises and daily lesson plans that it uses at each stage.

Four Levels of learning

The *BEC* program moves through four levels of learning - each one framed by the level of relationship it is possible for you to have with people in the community. As your ability to relate to people increases, and your language and cultural ability grows, the *BEC* activities and cultural focus at each level reflect this gradual increase.

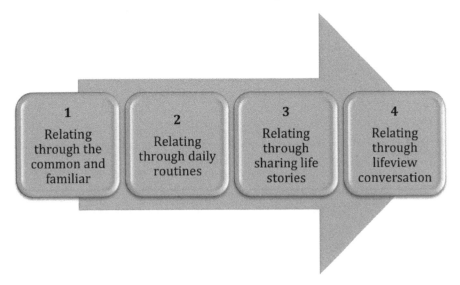

| 1 Relating through the common and familiar | 2 Relating through daily routines | 3 Relating through sharing life stories | 4 Relating through lifeview conversation |

Learning Activities for each level

There are only five major learning activities used by the BEC program:

- Participant Observation
- Listen and Act (for listening comprehension)
- Listen and Act with Speaking
- Working with Daily Routines
- Sharing Life Stories
- Lifeview Conversation

This is when the different learning activities are used throughout the program:

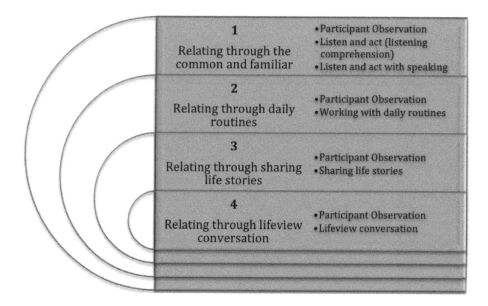

1 Relating through the common and familiar	• Participant Observation • Listen and act (listening comprehension) • Listen and act with speaking
2 Relating through daily routines	• Participant Observation • Working with daily routines
3 Relating through sharing life stories	• Participant Observation • Sharing life stories
4 Relating through lifeview conversation	• Participant Observation • Lifeview conversation

Daily Learning Plans

Detailed learning plans are included for each day of the program, designed to take a learner through profitable exercises for their particular stage and ability. Here is an overview of the Daily Learning Plans for each level:

Level 1: 50 Daily Learning Plans:

- *Participant Observation* learning exercises in common activities and settings in the community.
- *Listen and Act* learning exercises.

- Review and Recording exercises.
- Setting up and using a Daily Lesson Plan Notebook.
- Planning the next day's activities.

After plan 25, *Listen and act with speaking* exercises are introduced.

Level 2: 80 Daily Learning Plans:
- *Participant Observation* learning exercises in the community.
- *Working with Daily Routines* learning exercises with community members.
- Review previous daily routine exercises and Recording and reviewing texts
- Daily Lesson Plan Notebook.
- Planning the next day's activities.

Plans 1-40 will help you to understand descriptions of daily routines and activities as community members explain them to you. You will also learn to understand appropriate questions regarding these activities. Plans 41-80 will help you to begin to describe these daily routines and processes for yourself, as well as ask your own questions about them.

Level 3: 100 Daily Learning Plans:
- *Participant Observation* learning exercises in the community.
- *Sharing Life Stories* learning exercises with many different people in the community.
- Review and Recording exercises.
- Setting up and using a Life Perspectives Notebook.
- Reading and reflection on the four life perspectives that can help you as you observe life activities and talk with others about those activities during level 3:
  - What *communication* is taking place in the activity?
  - How is group or individual *identity* playing out in the activity?
  - What *rules for living* are being expressed in the activity?
  - What *relationships* are evident in the activity?
- Planning the next day's activities.

The earlier plans will help you to understand life stories as community members relate them to you. The later plans will help you to begin to tell stories yourself, both about the experience of others as well as your own life experience.

Level 4: 100 Daily Learning Plans:

- *Lifeview Conversation* learning exercises.
- Expanding and adding further questions to your Life Perspectives Notebook.
- Planning the next day's activities.

Earlier plans will help you to continue on from what you've learned in your *Sharing Life Stories* exercises of relationship building. In the later part of the daily learning plans, you will begin to include the life perspectives topics into your conversations. Further discussion questions are included to help you to explore these topics - you will make observation notes about the beliefs of community members that seem to be motivating their behaviour based on your conversations with them. This will help in focusing your attention toward your long-term goals and objectives.

 DISCUSSION POINTS

1. What did you learn through applying the Lifeview Conversation exercise?
- Was it easy to find two people willing to spend two hours of their time with you?
- What were some of the differences in the two people you had a conversation with? (E.g., was one easier to work with that the other, and if so, why? Were their answers to the same questions different and why do you think that is?)
- Are there any other reflections you have after doing the exercise?

 ACTIVITIES

1. Meet with the second person you planned to have a conversation with and do the Lifeview Conversation activity with them.

2. Listen to the recording you made of the conversation. Make notes of any further questions you would like to ask if you had another conversation with this person, and any interesting observations that you've made. Reflect on the four life perspectives and note anything from the conversation that lends support to, or serves as an example for any of the perspectives.

OBJECTIVES OF THIS TUTORIAL

This tutorial looks at the area of evaluating the proficiency of a person who is learning another language and culture.

Introduction

In previous tutorials we looked at the whole area of language and culture proficiency: what our goals are for proficiency and why, and what each level actually looks like in terms of functional ability (see Tutorials 4.17, 4.20 and 4.21). In this tutorial we will look at how to adequately evaluate a person's level of ability in a second language and culture and what are some of the factors involved in evaluation.

Why evaluate proficiency?

Many universities in Australia require a prospective student to meet a minimum required level in English speaking, reading, writing and listening, before they are allowed to enrol. Why? Because there is a minimal language level needed for a person to be able to effectively function in a university course: to understand the lectures, do assignments, interact with supervisors, engage with the written material, work in a group situation, etc. Someone at a level below the university's minimum required level of English simply would not be able to function in the role of a student in a course.

The Australian Citizenship Test includes an evaluation in English as well as questions relating to key Australian historical and cultural areas. The rationale given for the test is:

> To assess whether you have an adequate knowledge of Australia and the responsibilities and privileges of Australian citizenship. The test is also designed to assess whether you have a basic knowledge of the English language. English is our national language. Communicating in English helps you to play a more active role in Australian society. It helps you to take full advantage of education, employment and the other opportunities Australia has to offer.

So we could say that proficiency evaluation gauges a person's ability to communicate well enough to fulfill a certain function or role - in the first case above, as a university student, and in the second, as an Australian citizen.

Proficiency for cross-cultural church planting

Obviously then, it is important that a person who is wanting to effectively engage in cross-cultural church planting has reached a sufficient level of ability and understanding to fulfill that role. Let's look at some specific kinds of functional abilities and the level of understanding that someone involved in cross-cultural church planting may need. Depending on their specific role, they will need to have some or all of the following abilities:

In the area of relationships:

- Have developed relationships so that there are some willing to be influenced by them on a fundamental, worldview level.
- Have gained sufficient respect to have some people willing to listen to them.
- Have productive relationships in the community with translation helpers, comprehension helpers, and individuals to help with various aspects of the work.
- Have wide-ranging contacts in the broader community in order to gather data and make informed decisions about the literacy needs, and the relationships and the ability to convince people of their need to gain or improve literacy skills.
- Have built relationships with some who could eventually become part of their "Bible lesson development team".

In the area of cultural Insight:

- Have cultural insights into areas of acculturation, authority etc. in order to do pre-evangelism and contrastive teaching about these issues.
- Have cultural understanding of "conceptual frames" in order to be able to make informed decisions in initial translation attempts.
- To have formulated some conclusions about cultural themes as they prepare to teach.
- To have cultural insights necessary to predict the areas which will pose the greatest obstacles to foundational truths.
- To have an understanding of cultural illustrations they might use in teaching truth.
- Have the ability to begin developing key terminology (in conjunction with Scripture translation).
- Have the ability to monitor an audience for their degree of comprehension and acceptance of what is being taught.

In terms of language ability and communication skills:

- To have the necessary communication skills to engage in pre-evangelism discussions and then teach (in a more formal setting) the relevant foundational concepts from God's Word.

- Have a good understanding and ability in the language to make functional use of most aspects and genres, including discourse features.

- Have sufficient competency to make initial translation attempts; first drafting, comprehension questioning etc.

- Have the communication skills necessary to teach an initial literacy class, encourage students, respond to questions, begin to train new teachers, and to evaluate the effectiveness of the program.

- Have enough of a competency in language to begin drafting initial Bible lessons, check for comprehension, evaluate breakdowns in clarity, appropriately ask questions, deal with incorrect answers, and also to answer questions.

- Have sufficient proficiency in language to make possible the extemporaneous exposition of God's Word.

What kind of evaluation?

Because cross-cultural church planting roles require abilities in language, cultural understanding and also in the area of relationships, an evaluation should cover all of these areas. It should evaluate what a person can *do* - their functional ability in real situations - not just what they *know*.

Because of the complexity of second-language acquisition, no method of evaluation is foolproof. But, if an evaluation is based on sound principles, it should give the learner a good idea of the level they are at and what they need to do to reach their goal of being an effective communicator in their context. As well as letting the learner know their level of proficiency, one of the major goals of an evaluation should be to motivate the learner to continue to learn and give them a clear idea of where they should focus and how to overcome challenges.

Oral Proficiency Interviews

One element that is an effective part of a proficiency evaluation is an oral proficiency interview. This is in the form of a carefully structured conversation between a trained interviewer and the person whose speaking proficiency is being assessed. The interview is interactive and continuously adapts to the speaking abilities of the person being tested. The topics that are discussed during the interview are based on the interests and experiences of the person, plus the culture that they are learning about. Through a series of personalized questions, the interviewer gets a good idea of the learner's ability to handle communication tasks specified for each level of proficiency. The interviewer can then establish a clear 'floor' and 'ceiling' of consistent functional ability. Often people are asked to take part in several role-play situations as well. These tasks provide the opportunity for the learner to demonstrate other linguistic functions and cultural understanding. An example of a role-play task is:

The learner has a health problem (allow them to think up something appropriate) and calls the local clinic to make an appointment. The 'nurse/doctor/receptionist' (helper) asks them to describe their symptoms. Then they make an arrangement of the date, time and place for the appointment.

The four interviews shown on the website with Module 4 are examples of oral proficiency interviews. They are usually around half an hour to one hour long. When the interviewer is not a native speaker of the language, a local native speaker of the language takes part in the conversation and role play scenarios with the learner and gives help in correcting and suggesting more correct or natural ways to speak or act - the conversation is still guided by a trained evaluator.

An oral proficiency interview can give insights into the learner's ability in many areas, including:

- Vocabulary
- Grammar
- Pronunciation
- Fluency
- Linguistic tasks
- Socio-linguistic/cultural awareness

Other elements of an evaluation

As well as an oral proficiency interview, an evaluation can include a social activity, where the learner can demonstrate their ability in a real situation with local people. This might be a visit to a friend's home, a local community event or site, or a meal at a local restaurant - any place where the evaluator can see the learner interacting in a natural way in a local setting.

An evaluation can also include a discussion with the learner about:

- their procedure, time schedule, and any challenges they are facing
- specific areas of culture, to find out how much they know and understand
- their personal involvement in the community, how many people they know, the amount of time spent with them and in which activities, what they talk about, etc.

Benefits of proficiency evaluation

One of the obvious benefits of an evaluation is finding out if you are ready to function effectively in the role you desire to do, or if you need to spend more time learning first. Evaluations are often very encouraging for a learner who has been working hard to make progress, but who is not necessarily seeing how much they have gradually improved over time - regular evaluations can help them to see the progress they are making.

Evaluation also gives an opportunity for targeted input from someone with experience, to get a learner through 'roadblocks' and to help them to move on to more effective learning. Finally, it should provide the learner with a "snapshot" of how they are doing in every area and give them a clear idea of their areas of strength and weakness. A thorough evaluation will help the learner to adjust anything necessary in his learning process and to encourage him to continue in profitable activities - not just in language acquisition and culture understanding, but in his relationships with people.

? DISCUSSION POINTS

1. When people are learning a new culture and language with the purpose of doing cross-cultural church planting, there is a tension between the urgency of the task and gaining an adequate degree of ability in communication. Many people move on to 'doing ministry activities' before they are able to communicate clearly. What could be some of the possible consequences of doing this?

2. Many people who have never learned another language find it difficult to understand how long it takes to get to a functional level, culturally and linguistically. Others believe that God is able to 'make up' the difference when a Bible teacher doesn't speak in the heart language of the people or is not yet a clear communicator in the language. What is your view and how would you explain it to others?

➡ ACTIVITIES

1. Do the English test at: http://www.englishtag.com/tests/level_test_lower_advanced_C1.asp You can do the C2 and the More Advanced test too if you have some time. What are the specific areas of skill or ability that this test evaluates? List some of the cross-cultural communication skills that it doesn't evaluate.

2. Read the excerpt - available on the AccessTruth website - from the *Culture Language Evaluation Handbook, 2013*, (an evaluation handbook developed for cross-cultural culture/language evaluation). The excerpt will give you an idea of an evaluation schedule and outline of the evaluation tasks.

6.20 Other culture/language acquisition resources

This tutorial provides some information about other helpful resources that are available for Culture/Language Acquisition.

Introduction

There are many resources available for language and culture learning, and you will probably find some good specific helps in the particular context where you are going - relating specifically to the language and culture there. Some of your best resources may be found by speaking to others who have successfully learned the language and integrated into the culture and community.

The resources we have mentioned here are general language/culture learning materials and articles, and they are included because they are based, at least in part, on the same learning principles we value (below), and so might give you extra ideas or help.

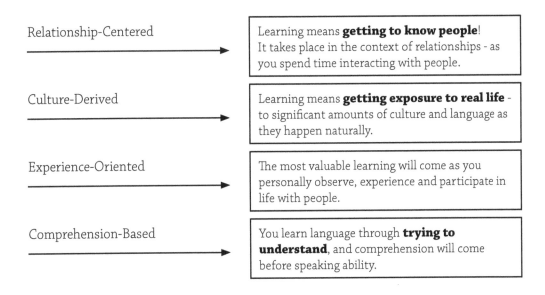

Relationship-Centered → Learning means **getting to know people**! It takes place in the context of relationships - as you spend time interacting with people.

Culture-Derived → Learning means **getting exposure to real life** - to significant amounts of culture and language as they happen naturally.

Experience-Oriented → The most valuable learning will come as you personally observe, experience and participate in life with people.

Comprehension-Based → You learn language through **trying to understand**, and comprehension will come before speaking ability.

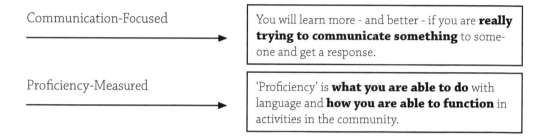

Communication-Focused → You will learn more - and better - if you are **really trying to communicate something** to someone and get a response.

Proficiency-Measured → 'Proficiency' is **what you are able to do** with language and **how you are able to function** in activities in the community.

The Growing Participator Approach

This is a language-learning program developed by Greg Thompson, a language learner and language coach based in the USA. The Growing Participator Approach is a systematic six-phase program - you can read about it on the GPA website. Have a look at the variety of articles and other materials in the Resources section as well:

http://growingparticipatorapproach.wordpress.com/

Sometimes the material can be quite academic in the way it is presented and how the ideas are expressed, but there are a lot of helpful things to read and think about, plus some practical sets of pictures, and other tools for learning.

Greg also has a Blog Spot for those using his approach, where you will find some helpful posts about various aspects of language learning:

http://growingparticipatorapproach.blogspot.com.au/

The Everyday Language Learner

This is a very helpful hub website with a number of resources: posts, ideas, videos, programs, books, and tips for learning language:

http://www.everydaylanguagelearner.com/

Summer Institute of Linguistics Language Learning Pages

Although some of the methods suggested in these pages represent a more grammar-driven approach to learning (rather than a relationship-centered, culture-driven approach), there are many useful resources and tools included here as well as links to other libraries of materials:

http://www-01.sil.org/lglearning/

CARLA (Centre for Advanced Research on Language Acquisition)

Although this site is for language teachers in the USA, it has some resources and links on integrating culture with language learning:

http://www.carla.umn.edu/culture/resources/

Cultural Bridge Productions

This page includes travelogues of various countries in Asia and interviews with people from those countries and/or people who have travelled there. It might give you a quick introduction to some aspects of culture and context:

http://www.johnsheaodonnell.com/CulturalBridgeProductions/index.htm

I Love Languages Pag

A comprehensive catalogue of language related links and websites related to a large number of specific languages:

http://www.ilovelanguages.com/

Why Warriors

A website dedicated to cross-cultural learning materials and links for Australian Aboriginal cultures, including some interesting articles and resources:

http://www.whywarriors.com.au/online_training/index.php

Ethnologue

Ethnologue is a site owned by SIL International, where you can find many resources to help you with general research of the world's languages:

http://www.ethnologue.com/

 ACTIVITIES

1. Look up each of the resources mentioned above, and familiarise yourself with the content and the different resources that are available.

Lightning Source UK Ltd.
Milton Keynes UK
UKHW050239210122
397469UK00003B/30